Color for Men™

Carole Jackson

with Kalia Lulow

Illustrations by Yuki Horikawa
Photographs by Ben Rosenthal and Jacques Silberstein

Ballantine Books • New York

Book design by Michaelis/Carpelis Design Associates, Inc.

Library of Congress Cataloging in Publication Data

Jackson, Carole, 1942–
  Color for men.

  Includes index.
  1. Men's clothing.   2. Color in clothing.   3. Grooming
for men.   I. Lulow, Kalia.   II. Title.
TT617.J33   1984   646′.32   84-45196
ISBN 0-345-31946-X

First Edition: October 1984
10 9 8 7 6 5 4 3 2

CONTENTS

This book is dedicated to

Alec and Megan Bartsch, my children, whom I love, admire, and respect.

Jean Halliburton, my mother, who loves, admires, and respects me. I love you, too.

Steve DiAntonio, president of Color Me Beautiful, whose warmth and acumen have made our company grow by leaps and bounds, and who made Color for Men possible.

Acknowledgments

Color for Men *is truly a reflection of combined energy, talent, and enthusiasm. To the following people who contributed so much I give special thanks:*

Joëlle Delbourgo, Editor-in-Chief of Ballantine Trade Books, who is not only a genius but a saint. Steve DiAntonio, for his logic, his love, and his tireless support. Jean Halliburton, for her literary skills (some of which rubbed off), and her broad shoulder.

Kalia Lulow, my co-writer, who endured spider bites in my basement guest room—for her talent and her fortitude! Nellie Sabin and Nancy Inglis, our editors, for pulling it together so beautifully.

Andrea and Alan Lentz, for writing the chapters on suits and body proportions; and Andrea again for her incredibly efficient handling of details. Ken Karpinski, for his knowledge of the men's clothing industry and his invaluable input. Louis O'Connor of Bloomingdale's for letting me pick his brain for two years. Dennis Lucier, for his expertise and advice on men's hair design.

Liz Singley and Sandi Wheeler for typing (and typing)—and late night laughter. Winnie Adams, for her perfectionism and proofreading.

Marie Kelley, Alexander White, and Mary Harz, for masterminding the photography shootings; Jacques Silberstein and Ben Rosenthal for taking these wonderful pictures; and Yuki Horikawa for his fine illustrations. Sylvain Michaelis, for his marvelous book design; Fred Dodnick, who worries about getting the colors right; and Jimmy Harris, who designed the wonderful cover.

Carol Brandewie, Tina Dyer, Errol Glidden, Norma Rios, Maria Caballeros, and Suzanne and Bill Doswell, who kept the rest of my life running smoothly while I wrote.

The wonderful staff at our headquarters and the Color Place, and the Color Me Beautiful/ Color for Men consultants who eagerly participated, especially David Kibbe, Roger Raley, Doris Pooser, Lou Marohn, JoAnne and Harry Robinson, Rubye Erickson, Nancy Matlin, Louise Wiltshire, Camille Oordt, Barbara Watkins, Carolyn Thurman, Earlene Herman, and Donni Betts.

YOUR COLORS

COLOR FOR MEN: WHAT'S IN IT FOR YOU?

- Do you look your best *all* the time?
- Do you project authority and confidence in a business suit?
- Can you combine your coat, shirt, and tie with complete confidence?
- Do you have sex appeal?
- Do you have the "right" thing to wear for any occasion all year round?
- Do you have a well-coordinated wardrobe—or a closet full of unmatched clothes?
- Do you hate shopping?
- Do you let your girlfriend or wife buy all your clothes?
- Do you shy away from peach, pink, or turquoise?
- Do you know what colors look best on you?

If even *one* of your answers does not please you, this book is for you. *Color for Men* is about color, image, and you. It's about using color to enhance your looks and your life. Yes, color is the secret to a good image. And what man doesn't want to look his best?

Color for Men is a scientific system, a way of dressing in colors that bring out the best in you. Why scientific? Your genes have determined the color of your skin, your hair, and your eyes. Only certain colors complement your natural coloring. When you wear the right colors, you come alive. Dressed in colors that work against what nature has given you, you fade away. I have seen a man change from a frog to a prince simply by changing his shirt!

The key is knowing which colors work best on *you*. The Color for Men system will help you discover your personal colors. You'll know exactly what clothes to buy—and what *not* to buy. It will simplify shopping and help you coordinate your wardrobe with ease. The beauty of the system is that all of your colors harmonize so you can mix and match easily. Best of all, dressed in the right colors, you'll look and feel terrific. At work, you'll convey power and elicit respect—and you'll feel sexier after hours.

Color for Men is based on the same system that inspired my book for women, *Color Me Beautiful*. To date, *Color Me Beautiful* has sold over 3 million copies and has been on the *New York Times* bestseller list for over three years. Obviously the system works!

Color Me Beautiful, Inc. is now a multi-million-dollar business. Our company has over 200 color and image consultants (male and female) worldwide. Our motto is excellence, our philosophy is service. In 1983, we launched the Color for Men division. In our men's consultations, we determine our client's colors and show him how to put color power to work for him.

We use the seasons as a way of describing your coloring and the colors that look best on you. Nature has done an outstanding job of arranging colors harmoniously, so we borrow from her to create a harmonious wardrobe for you. You are either a Winter, Summer, Autumn, or Spring.

The Winter man looks most striking in cool colors with sharp contrast, like the winter evening's dark sky and the pure white snow. The Summer man's coloring is most complemented by the cool, dusty colors of summertime—the blue-green sea, hazy white clouds, and grayed blue of the summer sky. Autumn is the man who looks best in rich, warm colors and muted earth tones, like the autumn leaves or a golden sunset. The Spring man's coloring is brought to life in the clear, fresh colors that come out in spring—the clear blues and ivories of mountain flowers and the bright green of fresh buds on the trees.

Now we are happy to share the power of color with you. This book will take you through the Color for Men system. First you'll identify your season. Then we'll provide you with a palette of colors that work together automatically. You'll learn how to assemble a well-coordinated wardrobe with something to wear for every occasion. The Color for Men system shows you how to combine a shirt, tie, and suit, how to choose accessories, even which hairstyle is most flattering to your face. You'll also find a tear-out section at the end of this book containing a summary of shopping tips for each season.

Color for Men is a total system. It's easy to use and it works! When you put it to work for you, you'll look great—and you'll feel great, too!

CHAPTER

2

RIGHT/WRONG

DATELINE: Monday morning, 8:00 A.M. Frank reaches into his closet to get dressed for an important meeting. He pulls out a gray pinstriped suit, a white shirt, and a burgundy tie. He dresses carefully, confident that his clothing projects the image he wants.

It's time to hit the streets. But alas, in the morning light, Frank looks as if he died on his way to the office.

Frank is an Autumn, and Autumns look distinctly awful in most grays. He cannot and should not try to wear that version of the standard business uniform. No matter what season you are, there are some colors that work for you, and some that don't.

Wearing the right color enhances your face. You look younger, healthier, handsomer, more vital, and more confident. Facial lines and shadows are smoothed away, your skin glows, your eyes sparkle. You project a positive image to both men and women.

The wrong color detracts from your face. It can make you look tired, sallow (yellow) or drain the natural color from your face. Dark circles, lines, and blemishes stand out. Wearing the wrong color may make your clothes overpower your face. People will focus on your clothes instead of you. Your capability and your authority are undermined because you do not project a harmonious image. In social and romantic settings, you may be turning yourself from a prince into a frog.

Don't panic. The good news is that actually you can wear almost any color in the rainbow; the tone, shade, and intensity are what make the difference. Knowing what colors look great on you lets you make subtle adjustments in your wardrobe that have enormous impact on how the world sees you—and on how you feel about yourself.

You can see from the photographs what a difference color makes. Your face has color (skin tone) and your clothes have color. They react to each other just like colors on a color wheel. Two colors placed together can bring out the best in each other—or the worst.

In a consultation, we show each man how he looks in each of his colors by holding a piece of fabric under his face as if it were a shirt. Some men never before realized how good-looking they are!

You are probably intuitive about your best colors. Look in your own closet. Isn't there a particular shirt you end up wearing every weekend, or a suit you feel especially great in (even if it is old)? And then there's that nearly new item of clothing that you never wear. Why? Most likely it's the color. It looked fine on the rack in the store, but it just doesn't work on *you*.

Men often have their intuitive color sense about what looks good on them stifled by their wives, their mothers, or salesmen, who instinctively try to dress you in *their* colors. Everyone favors his own best colors. If you rely on other people who don't know your colors to do your shopping, you'll end up with a wardrobe that is out of step with your natural color sense *and* clashes with your natural good looks.

Most of the popular corporate-image surveys were conducted in the East, where—particularly in New York—Winters predominate. While Winters and Summers do look their best in the usual business colors, Autumns and Springs, who are flattered by warm, golden colors, must find shades of navy and gray that both project a corporate image *and* work with their coloring. It's hard to look competent with a drawn, tired-looking face, yet many men undermine their image by adopting the "success" look without regard for what works for them individually. All men have the freedom to find their own power colors in their own best shades and combinations. On some, for example, brown looks best!

Frank (the man mentioned at the beginning of the chapter) was an executive who came to us for a consultation. He was wearing his dark gray pinstriped suit, white shirt, and burgundy tie. The clothes looked great, but Frank, an Autumn, looked terrible. We showed him how to find his version of "gray" and how an Autumn uses the right shirt and tie to pull off a navy suit. (Navy is not an Autumn's best color.) We changed his tie from burgundy to a shade of red that flattered him. Result: Frank had an image that was entirely appropriate for his job, but with added *personal* credibility.

David, an overweight middle-aged man, began to feel that life was passing him by. His wife started to tease him about his "mid-life crisis"—until she noticed he wasn't laughing. To give his self-image a boost, she coaxed him into having his colors done. Skeptical at first, David learned that he is a Spring. A modest sort, he wanted to keep wearing "safe" colors, but in his case, he needed to get away from white and dark blue and experiment instead with some more interesting, and more flattering, shades. David bought a new camel-colored jacket and wore it out to dinner. The response was immediate and dramatic. Had he changed his glasses? Cut his hair? Lost weight? Not yet. But soon, with the confidence he gained from learning his best colors, David found the impetus to do all three.

The effectiveness of personal colors applies to any man, whether he's a doctor, a plumber, an executive, a retired grandpa or a teenager. Test it yourself! The results are immediate. Buy a couple of polo shirts or T-shirts in colors that bring out your best, and watch the positive response you get from those around you. Try a new tie and shirt in your colors and give your working image a boost. It's important that you get feedback from others, since you'll find it difficult to be objective about your own appearance.

Once you know your colors, you will have the power to look good consistently, and to believe in yourself all the time. You really *can* color your way to the top.

wrong/winter

right/winter

Jacques is a Winter with olive skin, brown eyes, and dark brown hair. He looks best in crisp, cool colors. The camel jacket looks dull on him and gives his skin a yellow cast. Jacques' face comes alive when he wears a navy jacket, white and blue shirt, and navy tie.

right/spring

wrong/spring

Bob, a Spring, looks great in the camel jacket, ivory shirt, and tan tie. It complements his pink-peach skin, blue eyes, and light reddish brown hair. The dark navy jacket drains the color from Bob's face. He would look great in a brighter navy such as the one worn by Rick on p. 38.

wrong/summer

right/summer

right/winter

Terry, a Summer, has pink-beige skin, soft blue eyes, and dark ash blond hair. The bright polo shirt is too strong for his coloring. Notice how your eye is drawn to Terry's shirt before you see his face. Terry looks great in his medium blue shirt which is more harmonious with his Summer coloring. Even his eyes look brighter and bluer in his correct shade of blue.

Winter Jacques, whose skin, hair, and eyes are more intense, really comes to life in his royal blue polo. Compare Jacques and Terry in royal blue. Jacques wears the shirt; the shirt wears Terry! Jacques would look washed out in the medium blue shirt that so flatters Summer Terry.

wrong/autumn   **right/autumn**

Arthur is an Autumn with dark red-brown hair, hazel eyes and light peach skin. Although he does not look bad in Summer's blue-gray suit, he looks *better* in Autumn's chocolate brown suit and oyster shirt. The gray suit looks insipid on him, while the brown one brings color to his face.

right/summer   **wrong/summer**

Summer Terry is wearing the identical blue-gray suit on the left. This is his best "power" suit. Winter's charcoal gray suit and pure white shirt overpower Terry's Summer coloring so that he looks drawn and tired.

wrong/spring

right/spring

wrong/autumn

right/autumn

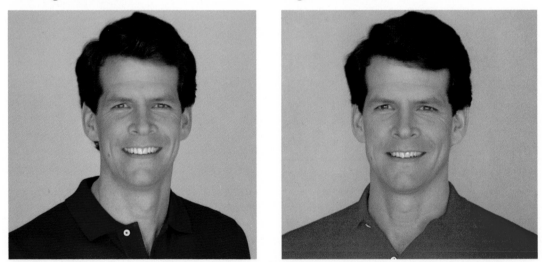

The burgundy shirt worn by Bob and Arthur in the left-hand pictures is wrong for both of them, but for different reasons. Bob's Spring coloring is overwhelmed by the dark color; its blue undertone is harsh on him. He looks younger, healthier, more handsome in Spring's orange-red. Arthur looks fine in the intensity of the dark burgundy color, but the blue undertone clashes with his peach skin, making him look pale and accentuating the lines under his eyes. His warm Autumn red on the right smooths his face and enhances his natural good looks!

3

THE SEASONAL PALETTES: THE COLOR CHARTS

In order to determine your own colors, look at the color charts in this chapter. The four seasonal charts are the building blocks of the Color for Men system. After you understand how the colors work and study the pictures of the men in each season, you can move on to the next chapter to personally test yourself and decide which palette is right for you.

UNDERSTANDING THE FOUR SEASONS

The Color for Men system uses the seasons to describe your coloring and the color palette that flatters you. Each season conjures an image of colors that everyone understands, and just as in nature, the colors within each seasonal palette harmonize perfectly. The four charts are *not* designed for use during the appropriate season of the year; instead, you belong to one season all year round. By using your season's chart as a guide, you'll be able to match your own coloring to the colors that are best for you, as well as put together a well-coordinated wardrobe in which your clothes go together effortlessly.

The Winter man looks best in vivid colors, dark colors, or very light, icy shades—say, a navy suit with a pure white shirt and red tie. The Summer man wears pastels and muted dark colors best; a blue shirt and blue suit are his favorite. Autumn is most harmonious in rich, deep earth colors, browns and russets, or muted gold-based shades from medium to dark. And Spring is the man most flattered by warm, golden colors, clear rather than dusty, light to medium rather than dark. A Spring man loves his camel jacket.

COMPARING THE COLORS

Winter and Summer are the cool (blue-based) palettes. The Winter chart has either blue-based colors or true colors (those with a balance of yellow and blue, black and white). The Summer colors have blue, rose, or gray undertones. Autumn and Spring are the warm (yellow-based) palettes. The Autumn palette is based on golden tones, and Spring's colors have clear yellow undertones.

The comparison table at the beginning of the charts shows some of the basic differences among the four seasonal palettes. First look at the different *shades and tones*. Notice how Winter's navy is clear and dark, Summer's navy is grayed, Autumn's is a marine navy, and Spring's is a bright, clear royal navy. Now look at the greens. Winter's is a true green, Summer's is a blue-green, Autumn's green is golden and earthy, and Spring's is a clear yellow-green. The reds for both Winter and Summer are blue-reds, because they are the cool (blue-based) seasons; the reds for the warm (yellow-based) Autumn and Spring are orange-reds.

Now examine the comparison chart for color *intensity*. Even though Winter and Summer are both cool, the intensity of their colors differs considerably. Summer's colors may be either clear or powdered (muted), while Winter's are all bold and intense. Compare Summer's light sky blue to Winter's deep royal blue. Autumn has strong colors, either vivid or muted, but Spring has only clear colors. Spring's palette can be bright or light, but never muted or extremely dark. Look at the difference between the browns and yellows of Autumn and Spring.

Now look at the color charts. Notice that a few colors are missing from some palettes. Only the Winter man can wear both black and pure white, but Winter has no brown or orange. Only Autumn has dark brown, but Autumn has no gray, pink, or purple. Summer has no orange. Spring has a little bit of every color except black and snow white. (*text continues on p. 40*)

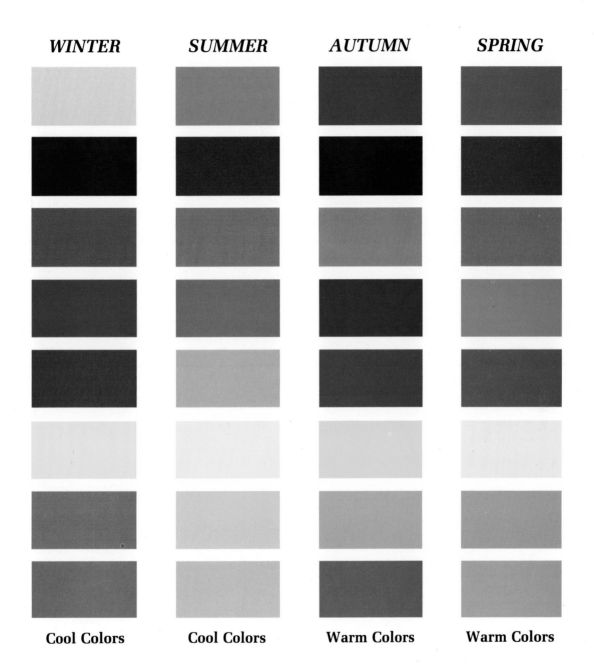

WINTER	SUMMER	AUTUMN	SPRING
Cool Colors	Cool Colors	Warm Colors	Warm Colors

You can wear almost any color; it's the tone, shade, and intensity that count. Winter's and Summer's colors are cool with blue undertones. Autumn's and Spring's colors have yellow undertones. One column is best for you.

WINTER BUSINESS/DRESS

Neutral Colors:
Suits, Coats, Pants

Light Colors:
Business/Dress Shirts

Navy	Charcoal Gray	Pure White	Icy Pink
Black	Medium True Gray	Icy Gray	Icy Green
Taupe (Gray Beige)	Light True Gray	Icy Blue	Icy Violet
		Icy Yellow	Icy Aqua

Ties: Colors from any category. Choose from Neutrals or Basics for a conservative look; any color for sportswear.

Shoes and belts (dress): Black, Navy

Shoes and belts (casual): Black, Navy, Cordovan (burgundy-toned), Gray. Add Taupe and White for warm weather.

Briefcase and other leather goods: Black, Cordovan (burgundy-toned)

Shopping guide: Winters are best in clear colors and high contrast. A Winter strives to stay sharp and should never wear muted, powdered tones. When shopping, think true, blue, and vivid; sharp, clear, and icy.

WINTER SPORTSWEAR

Basic Colors:
Sport Coats,
Slacks, Outerwear

Bright/Accent Colors:
Sportswear

True Blue

Pine Green

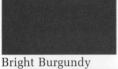

Bright Burgundy

Royal Purple	True Red	Lemon Yellow
Fuchsia	Emerald Green	Chinese Blue
Magenta	True Green	Hot Turquoise
Deep Hot Pink	Light True Green	Royal Blue

Blue-Red

Shocking Pink

WINTER MEN

Ben is a Winter with rose-beige skin, gray-green eyes, and silver-gray hair. He grayed prematurely, as Winters often do.

Danny has classic Winter coloring: dark brown hair, brown eyes and olive skin. He is especially flattered by the bright Winter colors.

Dean has black-brown hair and hazel eyes. Unlike most Winters, he has rosy cheeks.

Toshio's olive skin appears sallow if he wears the wrong colors. In clear colors, he looks healthy and attractive.

WINTER MEN

Dale is a fair-skinned Winter, with bright blue eyes and dark hair. He wears Winter's icy colors and dark, cool colors especially well.

Tim, unlike most Winters, has pink-beige skin. His eyes are a soft blue with brownish centers.

Neil has light gray-beige skin, green eyes with white flecks in the iris and dark brown hair. He wears all his Winter colors equally well.

Joe's dark hair, black-brown eyes and rose-brown skin are flattered by the high contrast in his pure white shirt and dark suit.

SUMMER BUSINESS/DRESS

Neutral Colors:
Suits, Coats, Pants

Light Colors:
Business/Dress Shirts

Grayed Navy	Rose-Brown
Charcoal Blue-Gray	Cocoa
Light Blue-Gray	Rose-Beige
Grayed Blue	

Soft White	Pale Lemon Yellow
Light Rose-Beige	Powder Pink
Powder Blue	Light Mauve
Light Periwinkle Blue	Lavender

Ties: Colors from any category. Choose from Neutrals or Basics for a conservative look; any color for sportswear.

Shoes and belts (dress): Rose-Brown, Black, Cordovan

Shoes and belts (casual): Rose-Brown, Cordovan, Navy, Gray. Add Rose-Beige and Soft White for warm weather.

Briefcase and other leather goods: Rose-Brown, Cordovan

Shopping guide: Summers wear soft Neutrals especially well and may wear both muted and clear colors. When you shop, think of blue or rose undertones. Even though you may favor your bright colors, you should strive for blends and subtle contrasts rather than extremely sharp contrasts. Your dark colors are always grayed.

SUMMER SPORTSWEAR

Basic Colors:
Sport Coats,
Slacks, Outerwear

Bright/Accent Colors:
Sportswear

Cadet Blue

Light Lemon Yellow

Medium Blue-Green

Orchid

Burgundy

Sky Blue

Deep Blue-Green

Mauve

Blue-Red

Medium Blue

Watermelon Red

Raspberry

Spruce Green

Periwinkle Blue

Pastel Pink

Soft Fuchsia

Pastel Aqua

Rose-Pink

Plum

Pastel Blue-Green

Deep Rose

SUMMER MEN

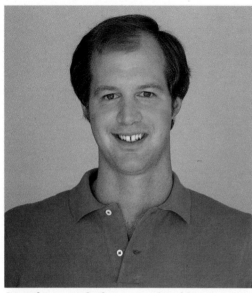

Steve has a pink skin tone, clear blue eyes and ash blond hair that turns slightly golden in the summertime.

Terry is a typical Summer, with pink-beige skin and blue eyes. White-blond in childhood, his hair is now a dark ash blond.

Steve looks great in a powdered pink shirt while Winter Tim (p. 27) looks best in icy pink.

Gordon's soft gray-blue eyes, pale pink skin and light hair are most complemented by the pastel shades of the Summer palette.

SUMMER MEN

With his ash brown hair, beige skin and hazel eyes, John looks especially good in his browns, which have rose, rather than golden, tones.

Bill's prematurely gray hair has a pearly white tone, typical of a Summer. Compare his hair to Winter Ben's (p. 26) silver gray hair.

Billy is a vivid Summer with dark brown hair, clear green eyes and deep rose-beige skin. He looks best in the brighter Summer colors.

Mel's soft blue-gray hair, blue eyes and pink skin tone are complemented by his blue shirt, blue-gray suit and blue tie.

AUTUMN BUSINESS/DRESS

Neutral Colors:
Suits, Coats, Pants

Light Colors:
Business/Dress Shirts

Charcoal Brown	Camel
Dark Chocolate Brown	Marine Navy
Coffee Brown	Olive Green
Khaki/Tan	Grayed Green

Oyster White	Light Peach/Apricot
Warm Beige	Light Periwinkle Blue
Buff (Light Gold)	Light Grayed Green

Ties: Colors from any category. Choose from Neutrals or Basics for a conservative look; any color for sportswear. Reds are acceptable for business as well as social wear.

Shoes and belts (dress): Brown, Dark Cordovan (brownish), Black (optional—to wear with Navy)

Shoes and belts (casual): Brown, Cordovan (brownish), Tan. Add Beige and Oyster for warm weather.

Briefcase and other leather goods: All shades of Brown, Tan, Beige

Shopping guide: Autumns can wear either muted or clear colors. You may use most of these colors as a general guide, but stick closely to the chart when shopping for your blues. Always think of golden undertones.

AUTUMN SPORTSWEAR

Basic Colors:
Sport coats,
Slacks, Outerwear

Bright/Accent Colors:
Sportswear

Forest Green	Yellow–Gold	Orange	Lime Green
Medium Warm Bronze	Mustard	Orange-Red	Moss Green
Rust	Pumpkin	Bittersweet Red	Bright Yellow-Green
Mahogany	Terra-Cotta	Dark Tomato Red	Turquoise
Gold	Deep Peach/Apricot	Jade Green	Deep Periwinkle Blue
Teal Blue	Salmon		

AUTUMN MEN

Autumn John has olive-green eyes and yellow-beige skin. The warm Autumn colors complement his coloring.

A light Autumn with strawberry blond hair, green eyes and peach skin, Stephen looks better in the muted colors of the Autumn palette.

Jay has teal-blue eyes, golden brown hair and peach-beige skin—a true Autumn.

Addison has charcoal black hair, dark brown eyes and light golden brown skin.

AUTUMN MEN

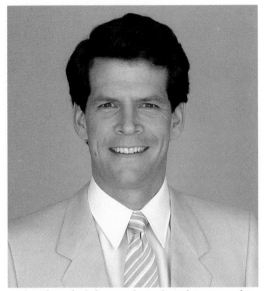

Arthur has dark brown hair, hazel eyes, and light peach skin.

Dale is an Autumn with blue-green eyes, peach-beige skin and brown hair with golden high-lights, who wears the rich Autumn colors well.

J. R. is a typical red-headed Autumn with olive-green eyes and a ruddy complexion.

Richard is a vivid Autumn: dark auburn hair, dark golden brown eyes, lightly-freckled golden beige skin. He looks best in high contrast colors.

SPRING BUSINESS/DRESS

Neutral Colors:
Suits, Coats, Pants

Clear Bright Navy

Chocolate Brown

Medium Warm Gray

Medium Golden Brown

Light Warm Gray

Golden Tan

Light Warm Beige

Camel

Light Colors:
Business/Dress Shirts

Ivory

Warm Pastel Pink

Buff

Light Clear Blue

Light Peach/Apricot

Light Periwinkle Blue

Ties:	Colors from any category. Choose from Neutrals or Basics for a conservative look; any color for sportswear. Red is acceptable for business as well as social wear.
Shoes and belts (dress):	Brown, Dark Cordovan (brownish), Black (optional—to wear with navy)
Shoes and belts (casual):	Brown, Cordovan (brownish), Tan, Navy. Add Beige and Ivory for warm weather.
Briefcase and other leather goods:	Brown, Tan, Navy, Beige
Shopping guide:	Springs need colors that are "alive." When you shop think clear, warm (yellow), and snappy. Your colors are the hardest to find because they must be clear— never muted—and not too dark.

SPRING SPORTSWEAR

Basic Colors:
Sport Coats,
Slacks, Outerwear

Bright/Accent Colors:
Sportswear

Light Clear Navy	Pastel Yellow-Green	Periwinkle Blue	Bright Warm Pink
Light Clear Gold	Bright Yellow-Green	Dark Periwinkle Blue	Coral Pink
Light Rust	Light Warm Aqua	Medium Violet	Bright Coral
Light Teal Blue	Clear Bright Aqua	Bright Golden Yellow	Light Orange
	Emerald Turquoise	Peach/Apricot	Orange-Red
	Light True Blue	Clear Salmon	Clear Bright Red

SPRING MEN

Joey has golden blond hair, clear blue eyes, and peach beige skin.

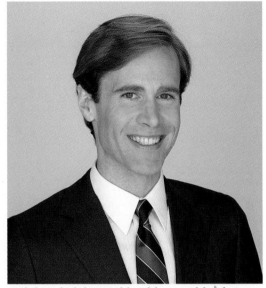

Rick has dark honey blond hair, golden beige skin, and dark blue eyes.

Tim has auburn hair, bright teal-blue eyes, and a ruddy pink-peach skin tone. He looks great in all of the clear, warm colors of Spring.

Lowell is a vivid Spring with golden brown hair, blue eyes, and peach-beige skin.

SPRING MEN

John is a light Spring with strawberry blond hair, turquoise eyes, and light peach skin. He looks great in the lighter Spring colors.

Cal's hair is red laced with warm, yellow-toned gray and his eyes are green. His light peach skin is slightly ruddy.

A typical Spring with fair peach skin and rosy cheeks, light reddish brown hair and blue eyes, Bob wears the pastel colors especially well.

John's gray hair has a warm, golden cast. He has pale blue eyes and ruddy peach-beige skin.

ANALYZING YOUR COLORING

Your skin tone, like your palette, is either cool (blue-based) or warm (yellow-based). You can wear almost every color; it's the tone, shade, and intensity of the color that make the difference. A yellow-green, for example, reflects differently on your face than a blue-green does. A powder blue has a different effect than a bright blue.

Studying the coloring of the men in the pictures will help you understand why one seasonal chart works best for one individual while another chart works best for someone else. For example, look at the difference between the Winter and Summer men. Winter coloring is stronger, with more contrast between hair, skin, and eyes. The Summer man has softer, less intense coloring. Even though both are from the cool seasons, a Winter man looks washed out in a pastel sky blue shirt, and a Summer's face is overpowered in bright, royal blue. In general, notice how much darker the Autumn men's hair and eyes are, compared to the lighter coloring of the Springs. Even a light Autumn requires deep, muted colors to enhance his earthy coloring. Bright Spring colors would look brassy on him. Spring, on the other hand, has a clear, lively quality to his skin and eyes, and looks drab in dark or muted colors.

UNDERSTANDING THE CHARTS

Each color chart is arranged to fit a man's wardrobe. Once you know your season, you can use your chart not only as a guide for buying clothes but also for choosing accessories, decorating your office, and even buying your next car! Notice how the charts are divided into *Neutral Colors, Basic Colors, Light Colors,* and *Bright/ Accent Colors* to help you organize your wardrobe and your shopping.

NEUTRALS are colors that go with everything. They form the foundation of your wardrobe. Select *overcoats, suits, jackets,* and *pants* from this group.

LIGHTS are for *business and dress shirts.* Shirt colors are important, since they are worn next to the face. Lights can also be worn in *sweaters* or *warm-weather slacks and suits.* Your shirt may be worn as a solid or with stripes or checks from any of your color groups. Here are some possible combinations for the various seasons:

Winter: White shirt with Bright Burgundy stripe
Summer: Soft White shirt with Blue stripe
Autumn: Oyster White shirt with Rust stripe
Spring: Ivory shirt with Blue stripe

BASIC COLORS are a little more colorful than Neutrals, but are still versatile enough to go with many of your other colors, and they add diversity to your wardrobe. Select *sport coats* from this group (also from Neutrals) as well as *sweaters*, *casual outerwear*, and *slacks*. These colors are often found woven into suit fabrics. Your favorite ties will probably come from this category.

BRIGHT/ACCENT COLORS are your chance to add a new dimension to your wardrobe in *sportswear, casual clothes,* and *ties*. Casual clothes and sportswear may be worn in Brights, either as solids or in stripes or other prints, according to your personality.

Although these categories suggest appropriate clothing from each section of the color chart, the divisions are flexible. For example, neutral colors, while most suitable for dress or business, may also be worn in sportswear. And ties may come from any category, depending upon your needs and personality.

The seasonal charts are designed to give you a complete range of colors, with something appropriate for every time of year and for every occasion. Some of your colors are suitable for wintertime, some for summertime. Your chart contains business colors, dress colors, sport colors, subdued colors and bright colors.

THE COLOR FOR MEN SYSTEM

Now that you've seen the color charts and the photographs, you may still feel you can successfully wear colors from all four seasons. Certainly you can find a few colors from each that might look good on you. Some colors are relatively flattering to everyone. But for two reasons you should not wear colors from a palette that is not yours. First, your season's colors are designed to be your *best*. Why look only good when you can look great? Second, the colors within each chart are compatible and are arranged to give you a coordinated wardrobe. When you follow your chart's guidelines, all your sport shirts will go with all your pants. Your ties will go easily with many of your suits and shirts. If you throw in an oddball color, you throw off the whole system.

To see how the system works, pick out a suit color from one of the charts. Now imagine each shirt on that chart with the suit. Almost every single light color works. Now choose another suit color and do the same. Do you see the versatility? Each suit can be worn with at least five shirt colors plus all sorts of shirts that include stripes, checks, or subtle prints. By adding five or six ties, you can have infinite variety (up to twenty different combinations) from just one suit, especially if it is a solid.

As you build your wardrobe using your own color chart, you will rapidly experience the true benefits of mix-and-match colors. You'll need fewer clothes, yet you'll have more to wear than ever before. You needn't be frustrated trying to get dressed in the morning, nor will you need to hang shirt and tie on the same hanger to remember what goes with what. Because your colors go with each other, your clothes will coordinate all by themselves.

Perhaps you are afraid you'll have to give up a color you really like. Don't! Keep it in your environment. Just don't wear it. If you're unhappy about having to part with a particular item of clothing, consider this: did you ever really get a compliment in that jacket? Or did the *jacket* get the praise? A true compliment is about you, not your clothes, and I promise you that as you wear your new colors and the compliments flow, you'll gladly part with a color or two. Eventually you'll discover that you don't even like that old color as much as you thought you did; you were probably led astray by fashion or by someone else's taste.

Perhaps you feel limited by the thought of wearing only one set of colors. In reality, however, you will have more options than you've ever had before. Most men are bored by conventional dress codes. Although you may make only subtle changes in your business attire, your sports and leisure clothes will now offer you a wider range of new colors. No need to be afraid of trying them—you know you'll look great!

The biggest bonus in finding your colors is the freedom it brings. Using your chart, you'll spend less time and energy shopping, yet you'll have more confidence than ever before in what you buy and how you look. You'll know what to look for and what to leave on the racks. You'll have a wardrobe of clothes you really like, with something appropriate for any occasion. Your colors will simplify your life, leaving your valuable time free for other pursuits.

Now go on to the exciting part—finding your colors!

DETERMINING YOUR SEASON: THE COLOR TEST

To find your season, you'll need to take a three-step test:

1. Assess your color history.
2. Evaluate your skin tone, hair color, and eye color.
3. Test yourself in colors (optional).

You can take this test by yourself, or you can ask others to help you. It's hard for us to be objective about ourselves, and other opinions can be helpful.

If you're not a do-it-yourselfer, you may want to skip this chapter entirely and go to a consultant for a personal color analysis. Information on consultations is included in the back of this book. Once you know your season, you can use the rest of the book to create an image that will truly reflect you.

STEP 1: YOUR COLOR HISTORY
Here we want to find key colors you feel you have consistently worn with success throughout your lifetime. This test is not based on image, but purely on flattering your face. Image is important, but it comes after you know your season.

Think of Your Most Successful Clothes

First, think of compliments you've received. Are people particularly responsive to you when you wear a certain suit or shirt? Don't dwell only on the clothes currently hanging in your closet. They may be right, but they may reflect this year's fashion rather than colors that truly flatter.

What colors made you feel good as a kid? Your intuition was probably better then, because you weren't yet influenced by the dictates of the adult male world. One word of caution: if your mother bought all your clothes and she is a different season, she may have dressed you in *her* colors all through your childhood.

Now think of yourself in your favorite weekend clothes. Because of the business dress code, men often pick the Winter or Summer palettes because these seasons contain the most "corporate" colors. When a man tells me he thinks he's a Winter, but all his casual weekend clothes are browns and beiges, I can be almost certain that this man is an Autumn, simply dressing in grays and blues during the work-week and wearing what he really looks good in on the weekends.

Select a Column

Now look at the groups of colors below and select the one you feel is most flattering to you. Think of all the colors in the columns as a casual shirt, turtleneck, or sweater. Pick the group containing the most colors that have brought you compliments all your life—even if you're tired of wearing them. This test is based on comparison. Each column may have some colors that you have worn, but do they all look equally good on you? Ask yourself, "Which group is *best*?"

WINTER	SUMMER	AUTUMN	SPRING
Navy	Grayed Navy	Dark Brown	Camel
Black	Blue-Gray	Rust	Golden Brown
Charcoal Gray	Sky Blue	Khaki	Light Clear Blue
Burgundy	Rose-Brown	Forest Green	Bright Blue
Royal Blue	Burgundy	Olive Green	Turquoise
Red	Pink	Dark Peach	Peach
Pure White	Soft White	Oyster White	Ivory

After you select one column, turn to that season's color chart in Chapter 3. Does the whole palette seem to suit you? If you feel pretty confident of your choice, go on to Step 2.

IF YOU'RE UNSURE

If you are deciding between two seasons, check out the color charts for both. Which one is more you? If you're stuck between two seasons, ask yourself the following questions:

If you are deciding between

Winter and Autumn, ask:
Does my face look better when I'm wearing a navy jacket, white shirt, and red tie (Winter) or, say, a brown tweedy jacket, beige shirt, and rust tie (Autumn)? Do I need clear, strong colors (Winter), or can I wear muted earth tones (Autumn)? Brown-eyed Winters sometimes mistake themselves for Autumns. A Winter looks good only in a very dark black-brown (not on Winter's color chart). All other browns are boring on a Winter.

Winter and Summer, ask:
Do I look better in a bright white shirt (Winter) or an oxford blue shirt (Summer) with my gray suit? Can I wear dusty pastel colors (Summer), or do these muted colors make me look washed out (Winter)?

Autumn and Summer, ask:
Do I look absolutely great in dark peach, rust, and brown (Autumn), or am I much better in light blue, blue-tone pinks and burgundy (Summer)? What color sweater would you buy?

Autumn and Spring, ask:
Do I look great in dark brown and bittersweet red as well as in muted colors like mustard and olive green (Autumn), or am I better in clear, medium colors like medium golden brown, clear red, light orange and light clear gold (Spring)? The Spring man will look drab in muted, grayed colors, while the Autumn man looks brassy in the clear, brighter colors that so flatter the Spring. If neither of these seasons seems to be working, try Summer. Sometimes it's that camel coat that led you to choose Autumn or Spring. Summer also has beiges and browns and a type of earth quality of its own.

Spring and Summer, ask:
Does my face look better in camel, golden brown, salmon, and bright blue (Spring), or in grayed rose-brown, burgundy, blue-toned pinks, and medium blue (Summer)? Remember it's your face, not your image, that counts here.

Spring and Winter, ask:
Do I look great in a camel jacket (Spring), or do I look *much* better in a dark navy (Winter)? Am I really terrific in ivory and golden browns (Spring), or am I better in white and dark colors (Winter)? A Winter man usually recognizes quickly how bad his face looks in camel.

STEP 2: EVALUATING YOUR COLORING—SKIN TONE, HAIR AND EYES

In this step you will examine your coloring to see if it confirms your choice in Step 1.

First, take a good look at your skin tone, hair color, and eye color. Study yourself in a mirror, preferably in natural daylight. Give yourself a close shave so your facial tone is not influenced by the color of your beard. A man with a heavy beard will have to look at other parts of his body. If you color your hair to cover gray or for any other reason, you will need to remember your natural hair color.

Your skin tone is the most influential factor in determining what colors look best on you. Because the skin is translucent, it is actually the tone just under its surface that determines whether your coloring is warm or cool. The *cool* seasons, Winter and Summer, have a blue or grayish undertone to the skin, while the *warm* Autumns and Springs have a golden or peach undertone.

Some people's skin tone is obvious, but for others the reading can be confusing and require a trained eye. Don't worry if you can't get a clear determination of your skin tone; it is only one part of the test and the other steps will give you enough information to make a decision. Comparison is helpful. Hold a piece of white paper against your palm or your stomach. Is your skin pink or even grayish next to the white, or does it have an ivory or peach cast?

Caution: Be careful not to confuse sallowness with a golden skin tone. *Many* people have sallow skin, which appears yellow on the surface regardless of the undertone. These people are often Winters and will turn even more sallow wearing golden-based colors.

In addition, ruddiness can be confusing. In a ruddy complexion, the capillaries are very close to the surface of the skin, giving an intense pinkness to the face, especially the cheeks and nose. This should not be confused with a blue undertone, as, ironically, ruddiness occurs most often in Autumns and Springs, the warm seasons. Here it's best to look at your chest and stomach.

On the following pages are more complete descriptions of skin tone, hair, and eyes for each season. Read only the season you selected in Step 1. If it fits, you can skip Step 3 and go on with the rest of the book. If it doesn't fit, then read the description of your second choice from Step 1. After weighing your answers to Steps 1 and 2, and looking at the male prototypes in the previous chapter, pick whichever season you feel most suits you.

Winter

SKIN: A Winter's blue undertone is often subtle and difficult to see. There are many varieties of Winters, yet they all need the same cool colors to look their best. The majority of Winters in the United States are those with gray-beige skin, ranging from light to dark, usually with no visible pink in their skin. Most olive-skinned people, blacks, and Orientals are Winters, though it is possible to find Orientals and blacks in any of the seasons. Many Winters are sallow, appearing yellow, and they misdiagnose themselves as Autumns. Wearing golden colors increases their sallow complexion, while the cool Winter colors make the sallowness disappear. A Winter may also have extremely white skin and dark hair. The white may have a visible pink tone, but more often does not. Winters usually do not have rosy cheeks.

HAIR: Winters usually have medium to dark brown or black hair, often glossy. The Winter man tends to gray dramatically, either reaching a salt-and-pepper stage or turning steely white. Hair that grays prematurely is a sign of Winter or Summer. Winter hair usually has an ash tone, although sometimes the hair will have red highlights visible in sunlight (this is not the metallic red seen in Autumn hair, however). Occasionally a Winter had white-blond hair as a child, but it turned dark by age five or six and is quite dark in adulthood. It is rare to see a blond Winter adult, but when it happens, his hair is often very blond and he is indeed a striking man.

EYES: Winter eyes can be black-brown, red-brown, green, blue or hazel, and are most often a deep color. The green or blue eyes of a Winter are distinguished by white flecks in the iris and often a gray rim around the edge of the iris. The hazel-eyed Winter usually has a brown smudge with jagged edges surrounding the pupil, with either blue or green extending to the outer iris. Occasionally a green-eyed Winter has a single thick yellow line going from the pupil to the edge of the iris like a single spoke on a wheel. In general, all Winter eyes tend to have a look of high contrast between the whites of the eyes and the iris. This clue is especially helpful if you are deciding between Winter and Summer, as the white of a Summer eye is usually much softer with less contrast to the iris.

WINTER PROTOTYPES: Burt Reynolds, Omar Sharif, Dustin Hoffman, Eddie Murphy, Richard Nixon, Tom Brokaw, Eric Estrada, Christopher Reeve

WINTER CHECKLIST

Check the characteristics that describe you:

Skin:
- _____ Very white
- _____ White with slight pink tone
- _____ Beige (no cheek color, may be sallow)
- _____ Gray-beige or brown
- _____ Rosy beige
- ___✓___ Olive
- _____ Black (blue undertone)
- _____ Black (sallow)

Hair:
- ___✓___ Blue-black
- _____ Dark brown (may have red highlights)
- _____ Medium ash brown
- _____ Salt and pepper
- _____ Silver-gray
- _____ White blond (rare)
- _____ White

Eyes: _____ Dark red-brown
___✓__ Black-brown
_____ Hazel (brown plus blue or green)
_____ Gray-blue
_____ Blue with white flecks in iris (may have gray rim)
_____ Dark blue, violet
_____ Gray-green
_____ Green with white flecks in iris (may have gray rim)

Summer

SKIN: Summers often have visible pink in their skin, so it is easy to see the blue undertone. Some Summers are very fair and pale and have little pink rings under the skin on the whitest parts of their bodies. The skin may have a translucent quality. Other Summers have rose-beige skin or sallow beige skin, making it hard to see the blue undertone. A sallow Summer makes an especially dramatic improvement in his appearance when he wears his cool colors. Black Summers have a soft grayish tone to their skin, and their skin is fairly light.

HAIR: As a child, Summer is often blond, his hair color ranging from white (towhead) to ash blond. While he is in his teens, his hair tends to darken, and by high school it has usually turned a light ash (grayish) brown. Summer blonds bleach quickly in the sun, so often a Summer man has brown hair in the wintertime and blond hair in summertime. If he spends lots of time outdoors, his blond hair may become golden, which can make him look deceptively like a Spring. (To judge your hair color accurately, look at the roots. If they are not golden, you are probably a Summer.) Brunette Summers also have hair with an ash tone, ranging from light to dark brown. Usually a very dark-haired Summer has extremely light skin, and visible pink in his cheeks. Occasionally a Summer has auburn hair (slightly red-brown) and can be confused with an Autumn. A Summer usually tans, while an Autumn more often burns. The Summer man's hair grays pleasantly to a soft salt and pepper, a blue-gray, or a pearly white. Gray is a cool color and blends well with the ash tones of his hair, giving him a distinguished look. (One caution: On a Summer man, a beard or sideburns often grow in red. Use only the hair on top of your head to do this analysis.)

EYES: Summer eyes are usually blue, green, gray or hazel, with a cloudy look to the iris. Often there is a gray rim around the edge of the iris, or the entire eye color looks grayed. Hazel eyes have a soft, grayed brown smudge around the pupil with edges blending into blue or green. The iris in a blue or green eye has a white webbing throughout, giving the appearance of cracked glass. Some Summers have soft rose-brown or grayed brown eyes. The whites of a Summer's eyes are creamy, in soft contrast to the iris, as opposed to a Winter, whose eyes have sharp contrast.

SUMMER PROTOTYPES: Prince Albert of Monaco, John Ritter, Paul Newman, Johnny Carson, Christopher Atkins, Merv Griffin, Jimmy Stewart, David Hartman, Alan Alda, Tab Hunter, Gavin MacLeod

SUMMER CHECKLIST

Check the characteristics that describe you:

Skin: _____ Pale beige with pink cheeks
_____ Beige with no cheek color (even sallow)
_____ Rosy beige
_____ Very pink
_____ Gray-brown
_____ Rosy brown

Hair: _____ White blond
_____ Ash blond
_____ Warm ash blond (slightly golden)
_____ Dark ash blond
_____ Ash brown
_____ Dark brown (taupe tone)
_____ Brown with auburn cast
_____ Blue-gray
_____ Pearl white

Eyes: _____ Blue (with white webbing in iris, cloudy look)
_____ Green (with white webbing in iris, cloudy look)
_____ Soft gray-blue

_____ Soft gray-green
_____ Bright, clear blue
_____ Pale, clear aqua (eyes change from blue to green, depending on clothes)
_____ Hazel (cloudy brown smudge with blue or green)
_____ Pale gray
_____ Soft rose-brown
_____ Grayed brown

Autumn

SKIN: Look for the golden undertone. Autumns come in three varieties: the fair-skinned man with ivory or creamy peach skin; the true redhead, often with freckles; and the golden beige man whose skin ranges from medium to deep copper. Many Autumns are pale and will look better in their darker or richer colors. Autumn men often sunburn and cannot get a tan. Autumns and Springs often have similar coloring, but the Autumn man usually has no cheek color, and the Spring does. On the other hand, some Autumns are ruddy and may look pink, but the pink is more peachy than blue. These Autumns look good in a few Summer colors, but really come to life in the true Autumn palette. A few Orientals and blacks are Autumns if they have a truly golden undertone, but most are other seasons.

HAIR: Autumn's hair is usually touched with red or golden highlights. It ranges from auburn to copper, strawberry blond to carrot-top, dark golden blond to warm brown. Some blond Autumns have hair often referred to as "dirty blond," and these men can easily be confused with Summer. A few swarthy Autumns have charcoal black hair. Autumn hair, except for a few auburns and dark brunettes, tends to have a matte rather than a shiny finish. The Autumn man usually does not gray dramatically because the gray may detract from his warm-toned hair. Once his hair has turned completely gray, it looks harmonious and has a warm, golden cast. During the in-between stage, he may prefer to color the gray with a warm tone as close to his original as possible.

EYES: Autumn eyes are usually golden brown, or green with orange or golden streaks radiating from a star formation that surrounds the pupil. Sometimes there are isolated brown specks in the iris. Some Autumns have clear green eyes, like glass, or deep olive green cat eyes. There are a few vivid blue (turquoise) and steel blue Autumn eyes that are marked by a teal gray rim around the edge of the iris. Occasionally an Autumn man has extremely pale blue or teal eyes, giving the appearance of a clear ring around the pupil. He is a pastel Autumn, looking best in the muted colors of the palette.

AUTUMN PROTOTYPES: Robert Redford, Dick Cavett, Red Skelton, Charlton Heston, Franklin Delano Roosevelt, Woody Allen, General Douglas MacArthur, William Marriott, Jr.

AUTUMN CHECKLIST

Check the characteristics that describe you:

Skin: _____ Ivory
_____ Ivory with freckles (usually redhead)
_____ Peach
_____ Peach with freckles (usually golden blond, brown)
_____ Golden beige
_____ Dark beige (coppery)
_____ Golden brown

Hair: _____ Red
_____ Coppery brown
_____ Auburn
_____ Golden brown (dark honey)
_____ Golden blond (honey)
_____ "Dirty" blond
_____ Strawberry blond
_____ Charcoal brown or black
_____ Golden gray
_____ Oyster white

Eyes: _____ Dark brown
_____ Golden brown
_____ Amber

_____ Hazel (golden brown, green, gold)
_____ Green (with brown or gold flecks)
_____ Clear green
_____ Olive green
_____ Steel blue
_____ Teal blue
_____ Bright turquoise

Spring

SKIN: Look for the golden undertone. The Spring man's skin is either ivory, peachy pink or golden beige, and he often has rosy cheeks or blushes easily. Some Springs are ruddy and can easily be confused with Summers because of their apparent pinkness. Even their knuckles may look purple. (If this describes you, look at the parts of your body that aren't ruddy to see the true tone.) Freckles, usually a golden tan color, come naturally to the Spring man. Other Springs have clear, creamy skin. Even if he has freckles, the Spring man's skin usually has a clear, bright quality. Black and Oriental Springs have light, golden skin.

HAIR: Spring's hair is flaxen blond, yellow blond, honey, strawberry, taffy red or golden brown. Spring doesn't have ash-tone hair, as Summer does. In childhood many Springs are blond, but their hair usually darkens with age. An occasional Spring has dark brown hair. Gray usually arrives in a yellow or cream tone on a Spring. If his hair is light, the gray often blends beautifully, making him look "blond." On a dark-haired Spring, the gray may detract from the golden tone of his hair. The Spring man may want to cover his gray until his hair is totally gray. Once the two-tone look is gone, his gray hair is beautiful and has a pale, warm, dove gray tone. Spring men often go from gray to a creamy white, a softly elegant look for them.

EYES: Spring's eyes are most often blue, green, teal or aqua, often with golden flecks in the iris. Some Spring men have eyes as clear as glass, giving the impression of a clear ring surrounding the pupil. Most Spring eyes have a "sunburst" around the pupil. Inside the sunburst you may see a doughnut tightly surrounding the pupil. Fibers radiate from the edge of the sunburst to the edge of the iris, much like the spokes of a wheel. Some Springs have brown eyes, but they are always golden or topaz. A Spring's hazel eyes contain golden brown, green and gold. A few Spring men have eyes of deep blue that appear to be steel gray from a distance.

SPRING PROTOTYPES: Ron Howard, John Davidson, Tom Smothers, Jimmy Carter, William Shatner, Michael Caine, Leslie Howard

SPRING CHECKLIST

Check the characteristics that describe you:

Skin: _____ Creamy ivory
_____ Ivory with golden freckles
_____ Peach
_____ Peach/pink (may have pink/purple knuckles)
_____ Golden beige
_____ Golden brown
_____ Rosy cheeks (may blush easily)

Hair: _____ Flaxen blond
_____ Yellow blond
_____ Honey blond
_____ Strawberry blond (usually with freckles)
_____ Strawberry redhead (usually with freckles)
_____ Auburn
_____ Golden brown
_____ Red-black (rare)
_____ Dove gray
_____ Creamy white

Eyes: _____ Blue with white rays
_____ Clear blue
_____ Steel blue
_____ Green with golden flecks
_____ Clear green
_____ Aqua

_____ Teal
_____ Golden brown

By now you should know your correct season. Do not be overly technical about analyzing yourself. *What looks good on you* is the best test of all. If you want to verify your choice or if you are still trying to decide between two seasons, take Step 3 and see yourself in the colors. Otherwise go on to Chapter 5 to learn how to use your colors.

(OPTIONAL) STEP 3: SEEING YOURSELF IN TEST COLORS

This is the at-home version of what we do in our consultations. Some people are genetically on the cusp of two seasons, and holding the colors under your face will help you see which season is *best*. You may look pretty good in some colors from one season, but on the whole look better in another palette. Never judge by one color alone.

This test is based on comparison. You should compare one color against another, perhaps several times, to see which is better. In the box below, locate the two seasons you are trying to decide between.

AUTUMN	or	**WINTER**	**SUMMER**	or	**SPRING**
Brown	or	Navy	Burgundy	or	Light Orange
Warm Beige	or	Pure White	Rose-Brown	or	Golden Brown
Rust	or	Blue-Red	Blue-Pink	or	Peach/Apricot
AUTUMN	or	**SPRING**	**SUMMER**	or	**WINTER**
Dark Chocolate Brown	or	Medium Golden Brown	Rose-Brown	or	Black
Mustard	or	Light Clear Gold	Soft White	or	Pure White
Khaki	or	Ivory	Medium Blue	or	Royal Blue
AUTUMN	or	**SUMMER**	**WINTER**	or	**SPRING**
Rust	or	Blue-Red	Black	or	Camel
Moss Green	or	Blue-Green	Pure White	or	Ivory
Teal Blue	or	Powder Blue	Burgundy	or	Light Orange

■ Gather the colors of the two seasons in question. Any solid-color fabric will do (shirts, towels, your wife's scarves, your child's T-shirts).

■ Give yourself a close shave so you can really see your skin tone.

■ Find a place with bright natural daylight, or bring a mirror to a window. Fluorescent light changes the color of both your skin tone and the fabric colors.

■ Ask for some outside opinions (people tend to favor their own colors, so ask more than one person in order to avoid individual bias).

■ Hold the colors under your face, using the combinations suggested in the box. Place the two test colors one on top of the other and hold them under your face. Look at the effect of the top color for a few seconds, then peel the top color off so you can see the effect of the second color. Repeat several times. Then go on to the next two colors. Remember, this test is based on comparison. One color may look okay, but the other will be better.

There are two rules:

1. **Be objective.** Try not to be influenced by your favorite and least favorite colors.

2. **Look at the face, not the color.**

Here's what to look for as you compare the colors under your face:

RIGHT COLOR

The color smoothes and clarifies your face. It minimizes the beard line, shadows, and circles under the eyes. It makes wrinkles or lines at the side of the mouth and nose blend smoothly into your face. It brings out a healthy glow in your skin. It makes your eyes sparkle. Your face pops forward, pushing the color into the background. The color harmonizes with your face.

WRONG COLOR

The color may make your face look pale, sallow or "dirty." It will accentuate a heavy beard, lines, wrinkles or shadows under the eyes. It will accentuate blotches or scars, if any. It dulls your eyes. It may age your face, especially if you are over thirty. The color will look too strong or too weak, in either case pushing your face into the background. The color does not harmonize with your face.

Here are the questions I am most frequently asked:

Can I be more than one season?

Not really. Some men are on the cusp of two seasons, but with testing, one palette will prove to be better than the other. Even if more than one color chart appeals to you, you are doing yourself a disservice to mix the palettes. Each chart is designed to create an automatically coordinated wardrobe, so "borrowing" from different palettes defeats the system. Remember, your genes determine your skin tone, hair color, and eye color, which in turn determine the colors that look best on you. Your best colors are not a matter of taste, but of fact.

Does my season change with a tan?

No. Your genetically determined skin tone doesn't change, it simply darkens with a tan or fades somewhat with age. The same seasonal palette will always be best for you.

When you are tan you can wear "wrong" colors more successfully, but why do it? You'll ruin your image and your wardrobe.

Does my season change when my hair gets gray?

No. However, once your hair is gray you may prefer to wear the lighter or softer colors from *your* palette. Your most flattering neutral colors will be the ones that harmonize with your hair—your season's grays and blues.

Now that you've assessed your color history, evaluated your coloring and possibly even tested yourself in colors, you should feel confident that you know your correct season. With this the pleasure of wearing your colors begins! Try out your season by wearing something you already own in your colors. Notice the response you get. The compliments you receive will confirm your choice.

5

UNDERSTANDING YOUR COLORS

Your seasonal color chart makes it easy to look good. But beyond coordinating your wardrobe, your colors also define your image and express your personality. Once you understand the colors themselves and have a *concept* of your season, you will be able to determine which colors within your palette are best for *you*, as well as to shop easily for your colors when you buy clothes. This chapter will focus on individualizing your colors, on using your colors in business and sportswear, and on understanding the colors themselves when you shop.

INDIVIDUALIZING YOUR COLORS

Your Coloring

By now you may be thinking, I'm a Winter with pale skin and John's a Winter, too, but with dark olive skin. How can we both use the same color chart as a guide?

Each season does encompass a wide range of people with different intensities of coloring, but your season's color chart may be interpreted to suit you as an individual. In our consultations, we drape each man in each color of his entire palette, using large pieces of fabric in order to see which colors are best. Most men wear all their colors well, but some men, depending upon their hair color and the depth of their skin tone, wear some colors better than others close to the face. If you are fair, some of the brightest colors may overpower your face and are best reserved for use as an accent in a tie or a striped shirt. By the same token, if you look best in the stronger shades from your season, mix your paler colors and neutrals with other, more intense colors. Use the pale colors as accent in prints and away from the face. *All* your colors are valuable to you because they give you infinite variety and the ability to build a coordinated and flattering wardrobe.

Your Personality

Your personality also influences how you will use your seasonal colors. Some men are comfortable only in conservative colors, even in sportswear, while others are more daring. Suit yourself. Each color chart has conservative as well as bold colors. All the colors will flatter you, but you will be most successful when you interpret your palette to reflect your personality.

Your Image

Your image is another consideration. Whatever your season, you can project the image you desire. Each chart provides you with the opportunity to be authoritative or low-key, sophisticated or casual, formal or informal. While one Autumn may prefer to dress with high contrast and project an image of power, another Autumn may want an elegant but understated monochromatic look.

Your Mood

And finally, each season can be interpreted so it reflects your mood. There are colors in your palette to express any mood, on a daily basis or even in yearly trends. You may spend several years in the mood for bright colors and then swing to a desire for calm ones.

To truly individualize your colors, consider:

1. *The intensity of your coloring.* Is your coloring strong or subtle?

2. *Your personality.* Are you conservative or daring?

3. *Your desired image.* Do you want to project an image that's authoritative or low-key, sophisticated or casual, formal or informal?

4. *Your mood.*

USING YOUR BUSINESS COLORS

In many professions, men want an image that conveys power and authority on some days and the cooperative team player on others. Many men work in offices and shops that require a degree of conformity to a standard dress code. A well-groomed, conservative image is the most effective. If you happen to work at a profession or in a business that allows more individual style—journalism, for example, or advertising—you can afford to be less conservative.

American businessmen have traditionally dressed in navy and gray, but not all men can wear the standard business colors with equal success. You need to adapt the image appropriate for your profession to your season so that you can both look good *and* project your desired image.

Keep in mind the following general rules to make your business dressing effective and attractive:

1. When your goal is to convey authority, wear your season's dark colors. Navy is the favorite, but Autumns may want to consider charcoal brown.
2. Wear your season's grays and/or tans when you want a lower-key image. A sport coat, if your profession allows it, is always less serious or authoritative than a suit.
3. Create the strongest *overall* image for you by wearing the right colors for *you.* You can make subtle adjustments to your business wardrobe without having to break the dress code of your work environment. Be sure to wear the right colors in your shirt and tie. You'll look better, and consequently others will see you more favorably.

USING YOUR COLORS IN SPORTS CLOTHES

The world of casual dressing ranges from sporty to natty, high fashion to preppie, rugged to sensual. Here is your chance to explore your colors and your character freely. The Brights on your chart offer a bounty of special sporty colors. By using them as accents or in combination with more subdued Neutrals and Lights, you can find new ways of expressing your style.

The safest way to wear your Brights is to buy your pants in neutral, conservative colors and try the bright or unusual colors in shirts. If you have an outgoing, unconventional personality, then you can go all the way with colorful pants and sport coats. You will still look tasteful as long as you stick to your palette because the colors will go together and will go with you. The only time you'll call negative attention to yourself is if you wear a daring color that is wrong for *you*.

If you want to try a color but aren't sure you will feel comfortable wearing it, buy it in an inexpensive T-shirt. When you get compliments, you will start liking that color!

For romance, think pink or peach, depending on your season. It's true! Women love a man in a pink shirt over candlelight. Try it!

Following is a basic explanation of each season's colors. Because it is difficult to print the color swatches 100 percent accurately, these verbal descriptions will help you understand the concept of your colors when you shop for clothes.* In addition, I've added specific information for each season on individualizing your colors—as well as how to use your colors for business clothes and sportswear. Read only your season, then skip to the end of this chapter, where you will find a chart comparing your colors with those of the other seasons. You may also want to review the color comparison chart on pages 84–86.

WINTER

When you shop, think: CONTRAST

SHARP

TRUE OR BLUE UNDERTONE

VIVID

ICY

Winter colors are intense. Your Winter image depends on sharp contrast and clear colors. A clear color looks pure and "clean." Never wear anything dull or muted, especially in ties. Look for the sharp navies and reds rather than the muted ones.

* *Directions for using the color chart to select clothes are in the Shopping chapter, pp. 199–203*

In general you wear dark colors, vivid colors, or very light, icy colors—no pastels for you.

THE WINTER PALETTE

■ White

Winter is the only season with pure white. A Winter man is never boring in a white shirt! You can also wear Summer's soft white (but *not* ivory or yellowish white), though it will not be quite as dashing on you as the bright white.

■ Black

Winter is also the only season who can wear black. You look great in dark colors, and any of your colors may get darker and darker until they look almost black.

■ Gray

Your grays range from charcoal to icy gray. They must be true grays, not yellowish or blue. Once your hair has turned completely gray, you may add blue grays to your palette.

■ Taupe (Gray-Beige)

Your beige is *not* tan-toned but gray-beige (taupe). When worn near the face, it must be light and clear. You may choose a darker shade in pants, shoes, and leather goods. Beige in general is a difficult color for a Winter to wear.

■ Blue

Navy blue is excellent on you. You may wear any shade of navy near the face except grayed navy. Your other blues are true, royal, Chinese, and turquoise, all deep or bright.

■ Red

Winter's reds are either true red or blue-reds, including burgundy. Your burgundy must be clear, sharp, and bright, rather than a muted or brownish tone.

■ Green

Your greens range from a true green to emerald to pine. Pine is similar to Autumn's forest green except that it has a blue cast rather than a yellow tone. You can see this difference by comparing the two colors side by side. Winter men who previously never liked green often discover that they love *their* greens.

■ Yellow

Your yellow is special. You can wear only a clear lemon yellow that does not verge the least bit on gold. Stick closely to your swatch when shopping for your yellow. It's hard to find.

■ Pink and Purple

Winter's pinks and purples are deep colors. The shocking and deep hot pink are less conservative, while magenta and fuchsia are quite sophisticated colors.

■ Icy colors

Icy colors are unique to the Winter palette. You can wear any of your colors in an icy version, including taupe and gray. An icy color is clear and sharp, like wearing white with a hint of color added. Your icy colors are blue, violet, pink, green, yellow, and aqua. Be careful not to accidentally buy a Summer's pastel shirt instead of your icy tone. You will lose the sharp contrast that brightens your face and makes your Winter image so effective.

Avoid all colors with golden undertones, such as orange, rust, peach, gold, yellow-green, orange-red, tans, and browns. If you must wear brown, choose a black-brown that is dark enough to wear with black shoes and belt. Avoid pastels and all dusty, muted colors. When shopping you may use your chart or color swatches as a general guideline for all colors except your yellow and taupe (gray-beige), which should be matched as closely as possible.

Individualizing Your Colors
The fair-skinned Winter man may find that soft white is better than pure white, and may also find that the icy and the darkest colors are better for him than the true, bright colors (see Dale, p. 27). Dark-skinned Winters may find that taupe and the light and medium grays are best when worn mixed with other, brighter

colors near the face (see Danny, p. 26). Some Orientals and olive-skinned men who are very sallow will not wear burgundy, fuchsia or their pinks as effectively as their other colors. A Winter with sandy brown or gray hair may add powder blue to his palette (see Ben, p. 26 and Tim, p. 27). Although it's a Summer color, a lighter-haired Winter can wear it.

Business Colors

Winters have the easiest time shopping for standard business clothes. *Black, navy,* and *gray* suits all look good on you. You may have trouble in the summertime, however, finding your version of a "tan" suit. Every now and then your *taupe* appears on the marketplace. Don't compromise. The usual tan suits look terrible on a Winter.

Your best business shirt is white, but the icy colors under Lights in your chart give you extra leeway for conservative yet stylish dressing. *Icy blue, gray,* and *yellow* are suitable for business or dress. *Icy pink* and *violet* are suitable for some business environments and are excellent for evening dress. *Icy green* is usually best with a sport coat. *Aqua* is best with a tuxedo or in a sporty oxford cloth shirt. You will usually find your icy colors in designer shirts. Most of the oxford button-downs are too dark and will look drab on you. The usual blue business shirts are best for Summers. If you can't find *icy blue*, then choose the lightest oxford blue you can find.

Your best ties come from your red family. Any *dark blue-red* or *bright burgundy* tie, solid or patterned, is an excellent business look for you, as is a *dark navy* tie, especially if it has some red or white accents in it.

A *taupe* trenchcoat is hard to find, as most of the beige trenchcoats are not your tone. If you can't find your gray-beige, consider *navy* or *gray.* Italian and German trenchcoats often come in gray.

Sportswear Colors

You can't beat a Winter in a *navy* blazer. But for variety try a *bright burgundy* or *pine green* blazer—preferably in a rich fabric such as cashmere or a fine wool. That will make you feel better when you pass by the camel jackets, leaving them on the rack for Springs or Autumns. Tweeds, even in your colors, usually don't look as good on you as solids. A pair of *gray* or *navy* trousers will go with everything in your palette.

SUMMER

When you shop, think: BLENDED

SUBTLE

BLUE TONE

ROSE TONE

The Summer palette gains its strength from a harmonious blend of tones, even in its most vivid shades. The Summer man's image is enhanced by soft contrasts and subtle color combinations. His dark colors should be slightly grayed (muted) in order to avoid looking harsh or overpowering his natural coloring. He can wear either clear or muted colors in his pastel and medium shades.

THE SUMMER PALETTE

■ Soft White

The Summer man's most flattering white is a soft (but not yellow) one. It is less "blue" than Winter's pure white.

■ Rose-Beige and Brown

Your beige must always have a rose cast, rather than an ivory or yellow tone. You can wear browns from medium to darkish as long as they, too, are rose-toned. Your browns are especially flattering if they are muted (grayed).

■ (Black)

Summer does not have black, as it is overpowering on the Summer man.

■ Blue-Gray

Summer may wear all blue-grays from light to dark, but should avoid true grays or yellowish grays. Grays devoid of blue will look dead on a Summer.

■ Blue

Your navy is a grayed navy, more flattering to you than a bright or black navy. Unfortunately, your navy is hard to find and you will often have to compromise. You may wear almost all other blues, light, medium, or dark, but not the extremely bright or royal blues of Winter. Your blues may be clear or muted, and your lighter blue suits will have lots of gray in them. When using aqua-toned blues, keep them soft. You can also wear periwinkle, a blue with violet in it.

■ Green

Your greens are all in the blue-green family, ranging from a light pastel shirt color to medium blue-green sport colors to a dark spruce green suitable for a sport coat or slacks. Your spruce green, like your navy, is a little grayer than Winter's. This spruce green is especially good on brown-eyed Summers.

■ Yellow

Summer's yellow is a light, lemon hue, ranging from pastel to a *slightly* brighter shade. Avoid yellows that are golden.

■ Pink

Your pinks are blue-toned pinks ranging from light shirt colors to medium shades to deeper rose and fuchsia colors. Although you may wear bright pinks, be careful not to buy the intensely clear and bright shades from the Winter chart.

■ Red

Summer's reds range from raspberry to watermelon to blue-reds. You may wear dark blue-red as well as burgundy and all wine colors. Unlike Winter, your reds may be either clear and bright or slightly muted.

■ Plum

Plum is your version of purple. It is a grayed purple, not as intense or as dark as the royal purple of Winter. Lavender, orchid, and mauve are wonderful colors for you, and they are easily found in both light shades for dress shirts and slightly darker shades for sportswear. You don't have to be careful when selecting these colors. Use your swatches as a guideline. If the fabric color blends with the swatch, it's yours.

Avoid pure white, camel, yellowish beiges, tans and browns, gold, orange, peach, orange-reds, yellow-greens, and black. Use your chart or color swatches just as a general guideline except when shopping for rose-beige and yellow, when you should match the color as closely as possible.

Individualizing Your Colors

Fair Summers with blond or light hair should keep the darkest colors of burgundy, spruce green, and dark blue-red as accents or use them in combination with a mellowing shirt and tie (see Gordon, p. 30). These dark colors may be too strong in a large amount right next to your face. Summers with dark brown hair are particularly handsome in the dark colors and in the more vivid colors from the Summer chart. This type of Summer just missed being a Winter (see Billy, p. 31). Brown-eyed and green-eyed Summers often look especially good in their browns and greens and should keep their blues and grays mixed with other colors for maximum impact (see John, p. 31). These Summers are close kin to Autumns, having an earthy quality yet needing cool, blue-based colors to flatter, rather than yellow-based ones.

Business Colors

The Summer palette, like that of Winter's, lends itself beautifully to the traditional business colors. Although it's best to find a *grayed navy* suit when possible, almost any navy that's not too blue and bright will do well for you when combined with your best shirt and tie colors. Besides navy, you have a wide range of suits in *lighter blue* shades. The *medium brown* suits that are most acceptable in business are great for you—as long as they have a rose tone. Your summerweight "tan" is hard to find. Occasionally you will find a suit in your *rose-beige* (your tan), but most often the tan suits will be for Autumns. Don't compromise. The wrong tan will look terrible on you. You do not wear black, but you can use your *dark charcoal blue-gray* suit to serve as your black. Because of your relatively lighter coloring, this gray will look dark and authoritative on you. Both your *soft white* and your *charcoal blue-gray* will appear as strong within your color chart as black and white do within the Winter chart. The impact of color is relative within the season and works proportionately with your coloring to create a powerful image. Be sure when buying a gray suit to choose a *blue-gray*. It's easy to spot the blue-grays hanging on the racks when you compare them to the true and charcoal grays.

Your business shirts are easy to find. The majority of ready-made pastel shirts are for you. All the *blues* as well as *yellow* and *rose-beige* are great for business, in addition to your *soft white*. In some business situations you can wear your *pink* or *lavender* shirts as well. You may even wear a *light blue-gray* shirt, especially if your hair is gray.

For ties, choose your *burgundy* and *blue-red*, either solids or patterns. Make sure these reds are slightly toned down. Use *watermelon red*, which is brighter, as a background color in a foulard tie. Your *grayed navy* and all shades of *blue*, mixed with white, gray, silver, mauve, or yellow, are great business ties for you.

Your trenchcoat, like your summer suit, may be hard to find in *rose-beige*. If you can't find one, consider *navy*.

Sportswear Colors

A *navy* blazer is a great look for you, especially with a *blue* shirt. For variety you might want to try a *spruce* green or burgundy blazer in the wintertime or a *medium blue*, *periwinkle*, or other pastel shade in a summerweight blazer. Many Summers, because of their softer coloring, look great in soft tweeds or even plaids in blue and gray, or brown and blue combinations. A pair of *blue-gray* trousers will go with almost everything in your palette. If you favor your browns, buy a pair of *cocoa* slacks for maximum versatility.

AUTUMN

When you shop, think: WARM

RICH

SPICY

GOLDEN UNDERTONES

EARTH TONES

Autumn colors can be either clear or muted, but always have warm golden undertones. A clear color looks pure and clean; a muted color is toned down by the addition of brown, gray, or gold. Most Autumns prefer their medium or bright colors slightly muted. The Autumn chart gains its power from an artful combination of blended tones with the more assertive, dark colors.

THE AUTUMN PALETTE

■ Oyster White

Your best white is oyster (beigish white). You may also wear ivory (a yellowish white) and the soft white from the Summer palette, but *never* pure white. It will make you look pale.

■ (Black and Gray)

You have no black or gray, so you will need to use dark charcoal brown as your black or charcoal gray and coffee brown as your gray. Coffee is any brown that has gray added.

■ Brown and Beige

All your beiges and browns are warm earth tones. Your dark chocolate brown and mahogany are rich colors. Camels, khakis, and tans are also good for you. Your bronze is an unusual color, flattering to an Autumn only.

■ Blue

A marine navy is the only navy that truly flatters the Autumn man. It is a navy tinged with teal or the color of the sea, and it's hard to find. You can wear any kind of teal blue, though the darker and richer the color, the better. Your turquoise is medium to dark and has warm yellow undertones. By comparing turquoises in the store, you can see that some are clear and bright (not for you), while others are yellower and slightly muted—again a full-bodied color. Periwinkle is a blue with a violet cast. In general, you look best in a deep periwinkle.

■ Green

Your greens range from dark forest green to olive, jade, and grayed greens. You can wear any green that has a golden tone, from subtle to bright. A light, grayed green is excellent.

■ Gold and Yellow

Your golden-colors are plentiful. Choose gold in a quality fabric or this color may have an inexpensive look.

You can wear any shade of gold, from light buff to mustard to a bright yellow-gold.

■ Orange

Your oranges include terra-cotta and rust colors, which are easy to find in all types of clothing. Your pumpkin and bright orange are sport colors, good in prints or in solids for the less conservative.

■ Peach and Salmon

Your best peach, apricot, and salmon shades are deep. Use the light versions mixed with darker or brighter colors to add oomph. Salmon is your version of pink.

■ Red

You may wear any red with an orange base, ranging from bright orange-red to bittersweet and dark tomato (more muted shades). Your reds may get brownish, resembling maroon. Avoid burgundy, as it is too "blue" and harsh for you, thus bringing out any lines in your face.

Avoid pure white, black, and gray. Avoid all pinks, burgundies, blue-reds, or colors with blue undertones. Keep your pastel colors, as well as peach, salmon, and periwinkle, a medium to dark shade when worn alone near the face (i.e., without the benefit of suit and tie). You may use your chart or color swatches as a general guideline except when shopping for navy and periwinkle, when you should try to match the color as closely as possible.

Individualizing Your Colors

A fair Autumn with light hair can be overwhelmed by some of the bright, clear colors such as orange and orange-red, so the fair Autumn man should reserve these for use in stripes and prints (see Stephen, p. 34). This is the Autumn man who just missed being a Spring, but who needs more muted colors than the ones in the Spring chart. Most dark-skinned Autumns will wear the more vivid colors better than beige, khaki, olive, or grayed greens (see Addison, p. 34 and Richard, p. 35). Autumns can be divided into three categories: the true Autumn, who wears all the colors equally well; the muted Autumn (usually light-haired), who wears the more subtle and muted colors best; and the strong Autumn (usually dark-haired or brightly redheaded), who wears the dark and vivid colors best.

Business Colors

Autumn colors do not fit the corporate mold. If you work in a business where the usual navies and grays are standard, you will have to shop more carefully. *Marine navy* is hard to find, though you may be able to find it through a tailor and have a suit custom-made. If you must compromise on your navy, remember to keep your tie and shirt in your season. You have a large selection of browns. *Medium browns* are highly acceptable for business wear and come in beautiful fabrics, especially in subtle patterns. For a larger selection than off the racks, go to your favorite men's store and look at the swatches in the books used for selecting custom-made suits. Your palette does not have gray. Use *grayed browns* to achieve the same look. A *charcoal brown* suit has a very similar look to a charcoal gray, and is especially powerful when coupled with a dark red tie from your palette. Subtle business *tweeds* look especially good on you, and they favor your colors— browns and greens. A little gray mixed in won't hurt, as long as the overall effect is yours. (How to tell? If it blends with your shirt and tie, it's yours.) Autumns are the lucky ones who get all the great *tan* suits in summertime. In addition, you'll find *greens* and *bronzes* in summerweight suits.

Business shirt colors are also harder for the Autumn man to find. Try to find *oyster white*. You can also wear Summer's soft white or Spring's ivory, but oyster will be your best. (I know one Autumn who dipped his white shirt in weak tea. It worked!) Your *beige, buff,* and *light periwinkle* are good business colors, and in some work environments you can wear *peach* and *grayed green.* Be careful when you are shopping for a periwinkle blue dress shirt not to buy powder blue by accident. Periwinkle has more violet in it and is much more flattering; powder blue will make your face look pale. You can easily see the difference when you shop, as powder blue will clash with the periwinkle of your chart or swatch.

Reds and navies are the favorite business ties. Be sure you select your *warm reds* and not the blue-toned reds or burgundies. A dark, muted *bittersweet* or *brownish red* is your best. A brighter red is okay if it is used as a background for a print. Use *navy* only as an accent, since it's hard to find your Autumn shade. Experiment with *browns, periwinkles, rust,* and even your darker *greens.* All are acceptable for business.

A trenchcoat for you is no problem to find, as most traditional coats are in your *tans.*

Sportswear Colors

In country, elegant or casual clothes, Autumn has the easiest shopping of all the seasons. Your colors are readily available, and the Autumn palette lends itself beautifully to sporty attire. In fact, the *tans* and *khakis* that are every man's ideal look good *only* on Autumns, so you can console yourself when you are searching harder to buy business clothes. You are dynamite in a *rich brown* tweed sport coat with texture, and if you are blond or honey-haired, you will shine in a *camel* jacket. Camel is not as good as a darker color on the brunette Autumns. Wear lots of leather and leather trim in any of your browns. A pair of *brown* or *tan* trousers will go with everything in your palette.

SPRING

When you shop, think: WARM

YELLOW UNDERTONES

CLEAR

LIGHT TO BRIGHT

ALIVE

The Spring palette is warm and energetic. The Spring man's colors are friendly and extroverted, as are most Spring personalities. You do not wear dark or heavy colors well, so strive for medium-dark to light shades. All your colors must be clear, which means they look pure and clean. Avoid muted (grayed down) colors, as you will look washed out in them.

THE SPRING PALETTE

■ Ivory (White)   The Spring man's best white is ivory, a creamy white. He may also wear Summer's soft white, but not Winter's pure white, which will make him look pale.

■ (Black)   Spring has no black, as it overpowers his coloring.

■ Gray   Your grays must be clear and warm (yellow undertones) and have a bright, crisp quality. Even in wintertime you should avoid dark grays. Light grays are your very best. A medium gray will look darkish on you because of your light coloring.

(Text continues on p. 81.)

WINTER FORMAL

With the Color for Men System, you have an automatically coordinated wardrobe, with fewer clothes, but more versatility. Here, the Winter man's navy semi-solid suit is shown with seven shirt and tie combinations. The four icy shirts are unique to the Winter palette: icy violet, icy gray, icy blue, and icy pink.

WINTER CASUAL

This gray, black, and white herringbone sport coat and charcoal gray slacks go with almost every color in the Winter man's palette. The Winter man's sportswear can be subtle or colorful, according to his personality.

SUMMER FORMAL

Look at the variety the Summer man can have with just one suit. This charcoal gray and blue semi-solid suit goes easily with seven different color shirts and ties from his palette for seven totally different looks (and more!).

SUMMER CASUAL

A beautiful gray-blue sport coat, a sampling of shirts in stripes, plaids, and checks from his palette, a couple of ties, some brightly colored polos and a pair of navy slacks give the Summer man an exciting wardrobe of casual to dressy sportswear.

AUTUMN FORMAL

This rich charcoal brown semi-solid is Autumn's "power" suit. It complements the Autumn man's coloring and harmonizes beautifully with the shirt colors. Notice how he can bring many colors into his shirts and ties—blue, peach, buff, beige, red, tan, olive, and rust, to go with one suit.

AUTUMN CASUAL

By choosing a brown tweed sport coat with multi-colored flecks, the Autumn man can have a variety of colorful, but harmonious looks. All the colors from his palette go together because all have a warm undertone. Autumn's sportswear has a rich and elegant look.

SPRING FORMAL

A camel-colored suit on a Spring man is elegant and versatile. He can combine it with shirts of ivory, buff, and beige for a conservative look or with yellow, peach, and warm pink for more color. The Spring color chart provides many tie colors that work well with this suit.

SPRING CASUAL

Spring has a wonderful array of colors for sportswear. With this golden brown sport coat and pants, he can wear any color shirt from his palette. For dressy sportswear, his jacket will go beautifully with the formal shirts. For casual wear, he combines it with colorful sweaters, polos, plaids, and stripes.

■ Blue

Your most flattering navy is a light, bright one. The next best is a darker but still bright and clear navy. Your other blues range from a light true blue to periwinkle blues, which are blues with a violet tone. Your aquas and turquoises are plentiful, ranging from medium to bright. A light clear blue is good on a Spring man. Avoid any blue that is too pale or powdered. You look best in blues with depth or brightness.

■ Brown and Beige

Your beiges and browns range from ivory to clear warm beige to golden tan, camel, medium golden brown, and chocolate brown. You do not wear dark browns or the grayed coffee browns. Be sure to avoid wearing any muted or muddy tans, such as khaki, near your face. You can wear khaki in pants.

■ Gold and Yellow

Your gold is light and clear. Buff and chamois colors are wonderful for you, as is bright golden yellow.

■ Red

The Spring man's reds are either orange-reds or clear reds. Dark reds are harsh and aging to your face, so they should be avoided. Spring may also wear light rust.

■ Green

Yellow-greens are for you, ranging from pastel to bright.

■ Pink and Peach

All shades of peach, apricot, coral, salmon, and warm pink are for you. You don't have to be the least bit careful when choosing clothing in this color family. You wear them from light shades to medium and bright ones. Warm pinks are the ones with yellow in them, easy to see when compared to blue pink.

■ Orange

Your orange is fairly light, never as bright as Autumn's orange.

■ Violet | Medium violet is your version of purple. Avoid darker purples; they will look too harsh with a Spring man's coloring.

Individualizing Your Colors

Most Springs have good color in their cheeks and therefore wear all their colors well. If you are a very fair, blond Spring, you will find that your brightest yellow and yellow-green are too strong in a large amount (see Joe, p. 38). If you are a dark-haired Spring, you may find that your camel and palest colors look best when mixed with a more vivid color (see Lowell, p. 38).

Business Colors

Spring has the hardest time assembling a business wardrobe because the Spring man's coloring demands medium to light colors and is easily overpowered by dark colors. Try to find the brightest, liveliest *navy* you can. Avoid very grayed navies. Your best gray is a *light warm gray*, usually found in summertime. *Medium warm gray* is as dark as you should go. Bear in mind that because of your lighter coloring, a medium gray will look dark on *you*. Color is relative. (If you must compromise on either your navy or your gray suit, be sure you wear a shirt and tie from your season.) Spring can wear *blue* suits in lighter shades than navy, as long as the suit looks alive rather than drab. You rarely find a *medium golden brown* wool suit fabric, but you will find *chocolate brown* as well as tweeds with golden tones. Again, in business suits, you may have to compromise and verge a bit into Autumn's browns—keeping your shirt and tie in your colors, of course. Like Autumn, you may need to have your business suits custom-made to take advantage of the wider selection of fabrics. In summertime you will find that some of the tan suits are clear and warm—just right for you. A *camel* summertime suit is great, if you can find it in a business style.

Business shirts are easy for you to find. Your *ivory, light warm beige, buff,* and *light periwinkle blues* are excellent for business wear. In addition, you may wear Summer's soft white (but not Winter's pure white—you'll look pale). Your *peach, apricot,* and *warm pink* shirts are acceptable in some work environments, and they're great as dress shirts for social wear.

Choose a red tie as often as you can. Because your *orange-red* is so bright, it will be more suitable for business when used as a background for a print. Your *light clear navy* is great too, as is a *light true blue* or *dark periwinkle*. Shades of golden tan, camel, or buff are fine for business, as is light rust or even teal.

A trenchcoat for you is a bit hard to find because most of the beiges are darkish and muted. Choose a beige that is light and clear, if possible. Also consider a brightish navy.

Sportswear Colors

Here you shine! What man doesn't want a camel sport coat? But you're the one who really looks terrific in it. Your golden browns and tans also appear frequently in sport coats, both as solids and in tweeds. Sport shirts for you offer wide selections in stripes and plaids, and Spring colors abound in brightly colored polo shirts. Most Springs enjoy their bright colors! A pair of trousers in beige or golden brown will go with everything in your palette. A special bonus for Spring is your perpetually youthful look—more than compensation for the fact that you have to work harder to assemble a business wardrobe.

COLOR COMPARISON CHART

	WINTER	SUMMER	AUTUMN	SPRING
White	Pure White	Soft White	Oyster White	Ivory
Beige	Taupe (Gray-Beige)	Rose-Beiges, Light to Medium	Warm Beiges Gold-Toned Beiges, including Camel	Light Warm Beige Creamy Beiges, including Camel
Gray	True Grays, Icy to Charcoal	Blue-Grays, Light to Charcoal	No Gray	Warm (Yellow) Grays, Light to Medium
Brown	No Brown No Tan	Rose-Browns Cocoa	Most Browns: Charcoal, Chocolate, Coffee, Mahogany Most Tans: Khaki/Tan, Medium Warm Bronze	Chocolate Brown Medium Golden Browns Golden Tans
Black	Black	No Black	No Black	No Black
Navy	Any Navy	Grayed Navy	Marine Navy	Light Clear Navy Clear Bright Navy

Blue	True Blue Royal Blue Icy Blue	Blue-Grayed (including Denim) Sky Blue Periwinkle, Light to Medium Cadet Blue Powder to Medium Blue	Teal Periwinkle Blues, Light to Deep	Light Teal Periwinkle Blues, Light to Dark Light Blue Light True Blue
Turquoise	Hot Turquoise Chinese Blue Icy Aqua	Pastel Aqua	Turquoise	Emerald Turquoise Clear Aquas, Light to Bright
Purple	Royal Purple Icy Violet	Plum Soft Fuchsia Mauve, Light to Medium Orchid Lavender	No Purple	Medium Violet
Green	Light True Green True Green Emerald Green Icy Green Pine Green	Blue-Greens, Pastel to Deep Spruce Green	Grayed-Greens, Light to Dark Yellow-Greens, Light to Bright Forest Green Jade Green	Clear Yellow-Greens, Pastel to Bright

	WINTER	SUMMER	AUTUMN	SPRING
Orange	No Orange	No Orange	All Oranges Rust Terra-Cotta Peach/Apricot	Light Oranges Salmon Peach/Apricot Bright Coral Light Rust
Pink	Shocking Pink Deep Hot Pink Magenta Fuchsia Icy Pink	Pastel Pinks Rose-Pinks, Medium to Deep Powder Pink	Salmon	Warm Pastel Pink Coral Pink Clear Bright Warm Pink Clear Salmon
Red	True Red Blue-Reds	Watermelon Red Blue-Reds Raspberry	Orange-Reds Bittersweet Red Dark Tomato Red	Orange-Reds Clear Bright Red
Burgundy	Bright Burgundy	Burgundy, including Maroons and Cordovans	No Burgundy	No Burgundy
Gold	No Gold	No Gold	Golds, Light (Buff) to Medium Mustard	Light Clear Gold Buff
Yellow	Lemon Yellow Icy Yellow	Pale Lemon Yellow Light Lemon Yellow	Yellow-Gold	Bright Golden Yellow

YOUR CLOTHES, YOUR STYLE

BUILDING A WARDROBE: CONTENT, COLOR, LIFESTYLE

It's time to put your colors to work and give yourself the pleasure of a wardrobe that works for you.

In order to build a wardrobe, you need to start with a foundation. I call this the Survival Wardrobe. The Survival Wardrobe is the clothing that every man needs to go anywhere and feel and look good. It is simple, well-coordinated, easy to shop for, and foolproof! When you combine your colors with an organized, modular approach, you've got assembling a wardrobe down to a science. Whether you are starting to build your wardrobe, correcting your current one, or making a change in lifestyle, the Survival Wardrobe makes sure you'll never be caught without something appropriate to wear.

THE SURVIVAL WARDROBE

Getting Started

The effectiveness of your Survival Wardrobe (and the rest of your wardrobe, once you get beyond the basics) is magnified when every single item is from your own color palette. Because you probably have some wrong colors in your closet to start with, your wardrobe will not be completely coordinated overnight. But if you buy *only* your own colors from now on, you will gradually produce the miracle of an automatically coordinated wardrobe.

Phasing out wrong colors can take a few years (those expensive suits!), depending on what you currently own and how much you have to spend. In the meantime, make your wrong-color suits and pants work by combining them with shirts and ties from your palette. Get rid of your unflattering shirts and ties, however, if your budget possibly allows. The colors closest to your face count the most.

You may find that there are certain items on the Survival List that you don't need. Fine. Cross them off. One word of caution, however. Think twice before crossing a suit off your list. It can take days, if not weeks, to buy a suit and have it properly fitted. Some of my young college-bound clients tell me they have absolutely no use for a suit. But I know of at least one young man who had to attend a good friend's impromptu wedding wearing his father's ill-fitting, wrong-color, stodgy old suit. He felt miserable. The secret of the Survival Wardrobe is owning it *before* you need it.

Obviously you will need more than one of certain items, depending on your lifestyle. We'll talk about quantity at the end of the chapter. For now the object is to identify the gaps in your wardrobe.

The Survival List

The Survival List is summarized on pages 97–98 and includes all the items you need to have a wardrobe that can take you anywhere. On the following pages, the items are described in more detail. After you read the descriptions, use the list as a shopping guide. Check off each item you already have in your color. This way you can easily see what you *don't* have. If you live in an area of the country where you have both hot and cold weather, you'll need to do this twice in order to assess both your wintertime and summertime wardrobes. If you have an item that's perfectly wearable but not in the right color, put parentheses around it to indicate you'll eventually phase it out. For now it will have to do.

The Survival Wardrobe

■ Suit

Your survival suit should be a three-piece solid-color neutral in a wool or wool blend fabric. The cut should be conservative—an Ivy League or updated American cut—and the suit should fit you to perfection. For maximum versatility, choose a dark neutral so the suit will be dressy enough for a wedding but also appropriate without the vest for business or less formal social events. For summertime, you might choose a lighter color and certainly a lighter weight fabric.

■ Sport Coat/
Blazer

Choose your most flattering neutral in a solid color. Use wool blends, corduroy, or ultrasuede for wintertime, and hopsacks, cotton blends, light-weight wool or linen-look fabrics for summertime. It's okay to buy a tweed or plaid instead of a solid if you feel it's more you, but a patterned sport coat will be less versatile with your shirts and ties.

■ Slacks

These are your dressy slacks. Buy a solid-color darkish neutral in a wool or wool blend for wintertime, and a light to medium shade in a lightweight wool blend or cotton/polyester blend for summertime. These pants must go with your sport coat and should be either lighter or darker than the coat in order to make a good contrast. Winters and Summers will probably buy their grays; Autumns and Springs, their tans and browns. Choose a plain style without pleats or gimmicks. These slacks can go to work or a party when worn with a sport coat, or to a football game with a checked shirt and pullover sweater.

■ Shirt I

This is your basic daytime shirt and should be in your season's white. (It's worth the extra effort for Autumns and Springs to search for their harder-to-find shades of white.

It really makes a difference!) Choose oxford cloth with a button-down collar or broadcloth with a plain collar, depending on your personality. Oxford button-downs are more casual. Summers and Springs could substitute a light blue shirt in this category.

■ Shirt II   For dressier situations, buy a fine broadcloth, plain collar shirt in white, white on white, or a subtle color from your palette. If the shirt is colored, make sure it goes with both the suit and the sport coat.

■ Shirt III   Your third shirt is more casual and can be worn with your suit (without vest), your sport coat, and your slacks. Choose either a solid color (oxford button-down is the most casual) or a subtle check, plaid, or stripe. If your sport coat is patterned, you will have to make sure the pattern in this shirt is compatible, or stick to a solid-colored shirt.

■ Tie I   Choose a solid tie in a deep basic color to go with suit, sport coat, and all three shirts. If you have bought a patterned Shirt III containing several colors, make sure the solid tie picks up one of the colors in the shirt. When possible, you should pick out the tie first and then the patterned shirt to go with it.

■ Tie II   This tie is patterned—a foulard (small repeat pattern), club, or paisley—depending upon your personality. The background of this tie should be the red of your season, or one of your deeper or brighter basic colors, with the pattern picking up the color of either your suit or your shirt (or both).

■ Tie III   Your third tie should be striped. Most men can wear some form of stripe, bold or subtle, depending upon personality. Some portion of this tie must pick up the color of your suit and, ideally, the color of your shirt as well. If stripes are too severe for you, then buy one more tie from the Tie II category.

■ Belt

Select a leather belt in a dark neutral that harmonizes with your season. Winters and Summers should find a silver-toned buckle, as silver is a cool color and looks sharper with your palette. Autumns and Springs should choose a gold-toned buckle to harmonize best with your palettes.

■ Business/Dress Shoes

Depending on your personality, buy either a leather oxford-type lace-up (with or without wing tip) or a dressy loafer. Choose a neutral color, preferably the same as your belt. These shoes should go with your suit and slacks above. Don't forget to buy mid-calf or knee-length dark socks so skin doesn't show when you're sitting down with your legs crossed.

■ Casual Slacks

These slacks are casual but not grubby. They can be cords, chinos, cotton/polyester blends, or even a nice pair of jeans, depending upon your lifestyle. You can wear your jeans or cords with your sport coat if you are a casual sort of guy. It's still best to buy your first pair of casual slacks in a neutral color.

■ Casual Shirt

For wintertime, choose a turtleneck, a solid or plaid flannel shirt, a long-sleeved polo, or whatever suits your fancy. For summertime, a short-sleeved polo shirt will do fine. Now you can have more fun with the color. Because you can wear Shirts I and III with your casual pants, you can afford to be less conservative with this casual shirt. Most people need to have more than one casual shirt, no matter what their lifestyles.

■ Sweater

Choose a favorite neutral or basic color to go with your nice slacks, your casual slacks, and all your shirts. The sweater can be a crewneck, V neck, or cardigan. In summertime you may want to skip the sweater, though a cotton knit or light-weight wool is handy for breezy days or cool nights at the beach.

■ Shorts

These shorts are not for active sports but rather for comfortable, presentable wear in hot weather. They can be short, mid-thigh, or just above the knee, depending upon your personality, your age, and your legs. Buy any neutral or basic color, or your season's white. A solid is best, but plaid is okay as long as it goes with the short-sleeved polo casual shirt. If the shorts are a solid color, you can wear them with Shirt III and roll the sleeves up partway.

■ Casual Belt

Your casual belt may be leather, but it's fine here to have a fabric belt, either plain or striped. If you decide on leather, choose a wider belt. Here's a chance to express your personality. Buy a cowboy belt if that's your thing.

■ Casual Shoes

Loafers, Top-Siders, Wallabees, or any casual lace-up will do here, depending on your comfort, age, and lifestyle. Tennis shoes and boots (Italian or cowboy) fall into this category. It is possible for some personality types to wear boots with their dressy sportswear on social occasions, but *never* in a corporate setting (unless you own the corporation).

■ Hackarounds

Everyone needs "old" clothes to hang around in on weekends, to paint the garage in, or whatever, and most people already have plenty of these. The point is to keep only those items that are in your colors. You may be spending 90 percent of your casual time in these clothes, so why look awful at home? T-shirts are inexpensive, so treat yourself to a new one and ditch *all* your bad ones. Hackarounds, by the way, are relatively sexy attire in the eyes of many women, and it's hard to be sexy in the wrong color!

■ Topcoat

Ideally you would buy a wool or cashmere coat in the dressiest neutral color in your palette. The collar could be trimmed in velvet or fur for maximum evening wear. In cold climates, this coat can be worn for business, though perhaps without the velvet. The lifestyle of most Americans has become increasingly casual during the past decade, so you may find that you can skip this purchase. If you attend a really formal event only once a year, you may prefer to freeze while running from your car to the occasion. A top-coat is a major investment, so if you do buy one, choose one in a classic style with no faddish details. You want this coat to last.

■ Trenchcoat

The trench-type coat is probably a must for every man. Buy one with a removable lining so you can use it year-round. It is a perfect business coat and raincoat, and functions well enough in the evening, except on really formal occasions. Color? Either the tan or the navy of your season.

■ Jacket

Choose a parka, fur jacket, wool-lined jacket, or peacoat for cold weather; a windbreaker, sweat jacket, or any light-weight jacket for warmer weather or climates. Choose any color from your palette. A neutral or basic color will go with all your clothes, but a brighter color may add some zip to your life.

■ Cold Weather Survival

If you have cold winters, you will need gloves, a muffler, and possibly a hat. Buy the gloves and hat in neutrals to go with the coat you wear most often. The muffler can be solid or plaid in any color from your palette that makes you feel good.

■ Sports/Hobbies

If you have a hobby or sport—such as tennis, jogging, skiing, or swimming—that requires special attire, don't forget to add these to your own personal survival list. Since shopping is so painful for some, you might as well pick up these needed items while shopping for everything else. Being organized keeps you from having to make many trips to the store.

■ Personal

Obviously a man needs underwear for survival, but I am assuming that these personal items—plus pajamas, robe, and slippers—are already part of your wardrobe, and get replaced from time to time out of sheer necessity. One tip: Have at least seven sets of underwear so you need to do laundry only once a week. If you send your laundry out, you'll need a two-week supply.

Finishing Touches

■ Tuxedo

I have not included a tuxedo in the Survival List because most men rent one on the rare occasion it is needed. If possible, rent a tuxedo in a color from your palette, but if black is the only color acceptable in a given situation, then at least pick a shirt in the most flattering white or pale color. Any man whose lifestyle involves formal functions as part of the routine would be well advised to buy a tux. If you can get away with it, buy it in your color: navy for Springs and Summers, charcoal brown for Autumn. Of course you lucky Winters will outshine everyone else in black. Springs would look best in a light, clear beige, if possible, but some situations will require traditional black, or a dark color at best.

■ Accessories

To complete your wardrobe you will need certain accessories. Be sure your leather goods, umbrella, pocket handkerchief, and other accessories are in colors from your palette. Why blow the harmony of your total look with one off-key item?

■ Fur

When buying fur, choose a color similar to your hair, preferably a shade lighter. The cool seasons should avoid red tones in any fur. Autumns and Springs may wear a golden- or red-toned fur if it blends with their hair.

■ Jewelry   Try to have your watch, rings, cuff links, tie tacks, and any other jewelry or metals in the hue best for your season. As with your belt buckle, choose silver or silver-toned metals for Winter and Summer, and gold or gold-toned metals for Autumn and Spring. Consider changing the buttons on your sport coat, especially if you wear jewelry that would clash. If you are a Winter or Summer and feel you must wear gold, choose a tone that is subdued and not too yellow. A bright yellow-gold will clash with everything you wear. Of course your wedding ring stays as is.

THE SURVIVAL LIST

Check off each item you already have in your color. Then shop to fill in the blanks.

	Cold Weather	Warm Weather
Suit	_____	_____
Sport Coat/Blazer	_____	_____
Slacks	_____	_____
Shirt I (basic daytime)	_____	_____
Shirt II (more dressy)	_____	_____
Shirt III (more casual)	_____	_____
Tie I (solid)	_____	_____
Tie II (patterned)	_____	_____
Tie III (striped)	_____	_____
Belt	_____	_____
Business/Dress Shoes	_____	_____

	Cold Weather	Warm Weather
Casual Slacks	_____	_____
Casual Shirt	_____	_____
Sweater	_____	_____
Shorts	_____	_____
Casual Belt	_____	_____
Casual Shoes	_____	_____
Hackarounds	_____	_____
Topcoat	_____	_____
Trenchcoat	_____	_____
Jacket	_____	_____
Sports/Hobbies	_____	_____
	_____	_____

Colors for the Survival Wardrobe

On the following pages you will find suggested colors for the major purchases on the Survival List. These are merely suggestions, showing how well everything goes together. Notice that all the shirts go with all the ties, and all shirts and ties go with the suit, sport coat, and slacks. Don't try to expand your wardrobe by mixing your sport coat with the pants from your suit. This is not a good way to stretch your budget, as suit pants usually are cut differently from slacks and are made from different fabrics, even if the colors are compatible.

The Survival Wardrobe consists mainly of Neutral and Basic colors. In addition, you will buy most of these items in solid colors. It may seem boring at first, but I assure you this approach will give you the most variety from the fewest items of clothing. As you expand your wardrobe to suit your lifestyle, you can add more colors and patterns to your closet.

WINTER
Sample Colors for the Survival Wardrobe

	Cold Weather	Warm Weather
Suit	Charcoal gray	Navy
Sport Coat/Blazer	Navy	Navy
Slacks	Charcoal gray	Taupe
Shirt I (basic daytime)	Pure white (oxford)	White
Shirt II (more dressy)	Pure white (broadcloth)	Icy Pink
Shirt III (more casual)	White with blue stripe	White with gray stripe
Tie I (solid)	Blue-red	Bright burgundy
Tie II (patterned)	Navy with white mini-dot	Navy with pink and gray motif
Tie III (striped)	Bright burgundy, navy, and white	Gray with navy, white, and blue-red
Belt	Black	Black
Business/Dress Shoes	Black	Black
Casual Slacks	Navy	Taupe
Casual Shirt	Burgundy, navy, gray plaid	Emerald green
Sweater	Burgundy	Lemon yellow
Casual Belt	Navy (fabric)	Dark taupe (fabric)
Casual Shoes	Cordovan	Cordovan
Topcoat	Navy	Not applicable
Trenchcoat	Gray	Gray
Jacket	Navy	True blue

SUMMER
Sample Colors for the Survival Wardrobe

	Cold Weather	Warm Weather
Suit	Charcoal gray	Grayed navy
Sport Coat/Blazer	Grayed navy	Medium blue (linen)
Slacks	Charcoal gray	Navy
Shirt I (basic daytime)	Blue (oxford)	Soft white (oxford)
Shirt II (more dressy)	Soft white	Soft white
Shirt III (more casual)	Sky blue and white stripe	Soft white with gray, navy, or burgundy stripe
Tie I (solid)	Burgundy	Deep rose
Tie II (patterned)	Watermelon red with sky blue and gray motif	Navy with gray and white motif
Tie III (striped)	Rose and light blue-gray	Mauve with navy and white
Belt	Black (or cordovan)	Black (or cordovan)
Business/Dress Shoes	Black (or cordovan)	Black (or cordovan)
Casual Slacks	Grayed blue	Rose-beige
Casual Shirt	Rose-pink	Medium blue-green
Sweater	Burgundy	Light lemon yellow
Casual Belt	Navy (fabric)	Beige (fabric)
Casual Shoes	Cordovan	Cordovan (or Rose-brown)
Topcoat	Charcoal blue-gray	Not applicable
Trenchcoat	Grayed navy	Grayed navy
Jacket	Light blue-gray	Grayed blue

AUTUMN
Sample Colors for the Survival Wardrobe

	Cold Weather	Warm Weather
Suit	Charcoal brown	Olive
Sport Coat/Blazer	Camel	Light tan
Slacks	Dark chocolate brown	Coffee
Shirt I (basic daytime)	Warm beige	Buff
Shirt II (more dressy)	Oyster white	Oyster white
Shirt III (more casual)	Peach/apricot	Light grayed green
Tie I (solid)	Rust	Bittersweet red
Tie II (patterned)	Rust, camel, and oyster paisley	Olive with tan and red motif
Tie III (striped)	Brown with rust and oyster stripes	Brown, camel, and olive
Belt	Brown	Brown
Business/Dress Shoes	Brown	Brown
Casual Slacks	Coffee	Khaki
Casual Shirt	Teal blue	Salmon
Sweater	Warm beige	Oyster
Casual Belt	Tan (fabric)	Tan (fabric)
Casual Shoes	Cordovan	Tan
Topcoat	Camel	Not applicable
Trenchcoat	Khaki	Khaki
Jacket	Mahogany	Coffee

SPRING
Sample Colors for the Survival Wardrobe

	Cold Weather	Warm Weather
Suit	Bright navy	Light warm beige
Sport Coat/Blazer	Camel	Light clear navy
Slacks	Medium golden brown	Light tan/camel
Shirt I (basic daytime)	Ivory (oxford)	Light periwinkle blue
Shirt II (more dressy)	Ivory (broadcloth)	Ivory
Shirt III (more casual)	Soft white with light rust stripe	Warm pastel pink
Tie I (solid)	Light rust	Navy (must blend with blazer)
Tie II (patterned)	Orange-red with navy and ivory motif	Clear bright red with beige and periwinkle motif
Tie III (striped)	Navy, rust, ivory, and camel	Navy, clear red, ivory, tan
Belt	Cordovan	Cordovan
Business/Dress Shoes	Cordovan	Cordovan
Casual Slacks	Light clear navy	Light warm beige
Casual Shirt	Light clear gold	Peach
Sweater	Apricot	Light periwinkle blue
Casual Belt	Navy (fabric)	Tan (fabric)
Casual Shoes	Brown	Tan
Topcoat	Camel	Not applicable
Trenchcoat	Light warm beige	Light warm beige
Jacket	Medium golden brown	Light true blue

BEYOND SURVIVAL: YOUR LIFESTYLE

After you have the essentials, you will need to expand certain categories according to your lifestyle. The Survival Wardrobe applies to any man, but your own situation determines what you need to be comfortably outfitted beyond survival.

For the sake of determining quantity, I've identified four lifestyles:

1. The Corporate Man: Suit Every Day
2. The Professional Man: Suit or Sport Coat Every Day
3. The Casual Man
4. The Man in Uniform

See what quantity of each item you need to keep your life running smoothly, and write the numbers on your Survival List, which then becomes your ideal shopping guide.

The Corporate Man: Suit Every Day

You are the man whose job requires you to wear a suit to work every day. You'll need six suits (at least three solids), twelve shirts, and ten to fifteen ties, plus one or two sport coats and one or two slacks for social wear. The suit-every-day man often has a big gap in his wardrobe—plenty of suits, a pair of jeans, but nothing in between. Buy two pairs of nice casual slacks and at least four casual shirts. And don't forget some casual shoes to augment your wing tips and your sneakers. You're used to being dressed up all the time, so pay special attention to completing your casual wardrobe.

The Professional Man: Suit or Sport Coat Every Day

Your job allows you the flexibility of wearing either a suit or a sport coat to work. Buy three suits (two solids), three sport coats, three pairs of slacks, twelve shirts and ten to fifteen ties. Like the corporate man, you need at least two pairs of casual slacks, four casual shirts, and a pair of casual shoes for weekends or evenings that require more than a pair of jeans.

The Casual Man

You may be retired or you may have a job that calls for casual clothes every day. Buy six pairs of casual slacks (at least half should be washable), twelve casual shirts, and two pairs of casual shoes. If your job or daily life allows for jeans and T-shirts, include them in the casual wear suggested. Since you're wearing these every day, be sure they are "new" and clean. There's a big difference between clean, pressed jeans and ratty jeans and T-shirts with holes in them. To complete your wardrobe, add one suit (solid color) for dress, two sport coats and two slacks for social wear, and six shirts and six to ten ties for both.

The Man in Uniform

You may be in the military or you may work somewhere that requires a uniform. Whatever the case, your work clothes are taken care of and you probably ought to own one clean uniform for each day of the week. You need one solid-color suit for dressy occasions and one or two sport coats and slacks for social events. In addition to your jeans, T-shirts, and other hackarounds, add two casual slacks, four casual shirts, and a pair of nice casual shoes to complete your off-hours wardrobe. If you "retire" from your uniformed job, you will need to reevaluate your quantities according to your new lifestyle. It's easy. Just pick another category and follow the guidelines for it.

Now that you know what you really need, you'll be surprised at how easy it is to shop. Remember, shopping ahead of need is the secret to a successful wardrobe—and an organized life! Whatever your lifestyle, with a plan and your color palette, you can now fill the gaps in your wardrobe and have clothes that really work for you.

YOUR BODY PROPORTIONS

Before shopping for a suit, sport coat, slacks, or shirt, you need to be aware of the overall proportions of your body. Are your arms short? Are you high-waisted? Are your shoulders and hips in proportion? Once you understand your body, you can make cut, style, and fit work for you to disguise your flaws and create a balanced look.

Since few of us are perfectly proportioned, our goal is to create the *illusion* of perfection. Basic to the illusion is a key principle of design: the eye rests where a line stops. By modifying the lines of your clothes, you can, for example, visually lengthen short legs, diminish a prominent seat, or widen narrow shoulders. A good tailor can make your clothes fit, but only you—by choosing your apparel intelligently—can make line, style, and cut work to your best advantage.

DETERMINING YOUR PROPORTIONS

Stand in front of a full-length mirror so you can examine your overall body harmony. Look at yourself objectively. You may wish to have a tape measure handy and a friend to help you.

On the next page is a Body Checklist showing you the key areas of your body that affect your overall look. After you have read the short explanations that follow, measure and study yourself, then fill in the chart.

BODY CHECKLIST

Height: _____ tall, _____ average, _____ short

Weight: _____ heavy, _____ average, _____ thin

Shoulder/hip proportion: _____ shoulders much wider than hips
_____ good proportion
_____ hips even with or wider than shoulders

Slope of shoulders: _____ tapered, _____ average, _____ square

One shoulder higher: _____ yes, _____ no

Leg length from hip to floor: _____ inches _____ long legs
_____ short legs
_____ average proportion

Waist: _____ high, _____ low, _____ average proportion

Neck: _____ long, _____ short, _____ average proportion

Arms: _____ long, _____ short, _____ average proportion

One arm longer: _____ yes, _____ no

Upper back: _____ straight, _____ round

Seat: _____ prominent, _____ flat, _____ average

Height/Weight

Everyone has a different personal ideal concerning height and weight. In general, 5 feet 9 inches to 5 feet 11 inches is average; 6 feet and over is tall; 5 feet 8 inches and under is short. In many instances, actual weight and height are not as important as the relationship of the body parts to the whole. However, if you want to appear taller, shorter, heavier, or thinner, there are ways of creating the illusion of a different body size, which we will discuss later.

Shoulder/Hip Proportion

Visually compare the width of your shoulders to that of your hips. A man's shoulders are usually wider than his hips. If your shoulders extend unusually far beyond your hipline, however, you may appear top-heavy. You will also look unbalanced if your hips are equal to or wider than your shoulders.

The 3 Body Types

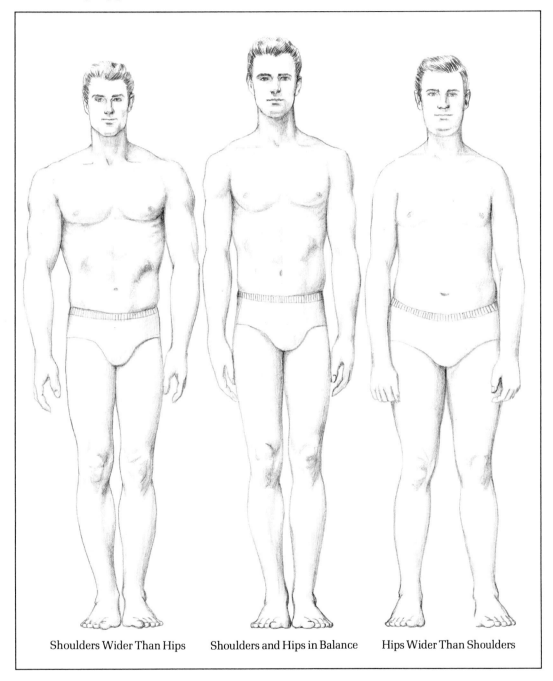

Shoulders Wider Than Hips   Shoulders and Hips in Balance   Hips Wider Than Shoulders

Shoulder Slope Facing forward, look at the slope of your shoulders. The average person has a two-inch drop from the base of the neck to the outer edge of the shoulder. If you have less than a two-inch drop, you have square shoulders; more, and your shoulders are tapered. Check also to see if one shoulder is markedly higher than the other.

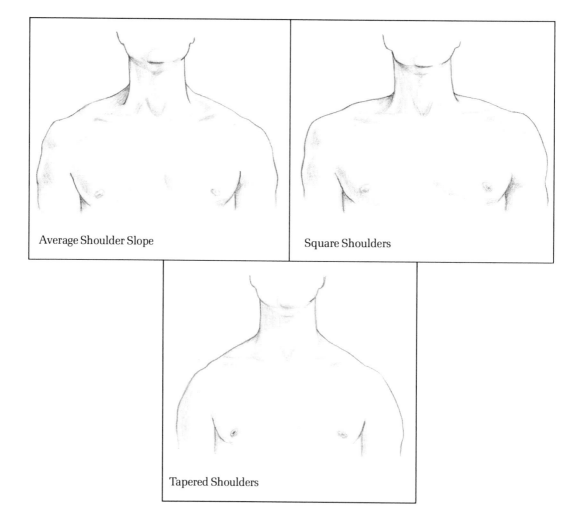

Average Shoulder Slope

Square Shoulders

Tapered Shoulders

**Leg/Torso
Proportion**

In a perfectly proportioned body, the legs make up half of the total height. Measure the length of your leg from hip joint to floor. (If you have trouble locating your hip joint, just lift your leg. Where your trouser breaks at the hip is the joint.) Compare the length of your leg to your overall height to determine if your legs are short, long, or in proportion. One inch either way is still considered average.

Waist/Body Proportion

First look at your total height, then look at your waistline (when belted). Does your waist seem especially high or low, or does it strike a pleasing proportion to your height? Many people with long legs tend to be high-waisted; short legs often contribute to a low-waisted look.

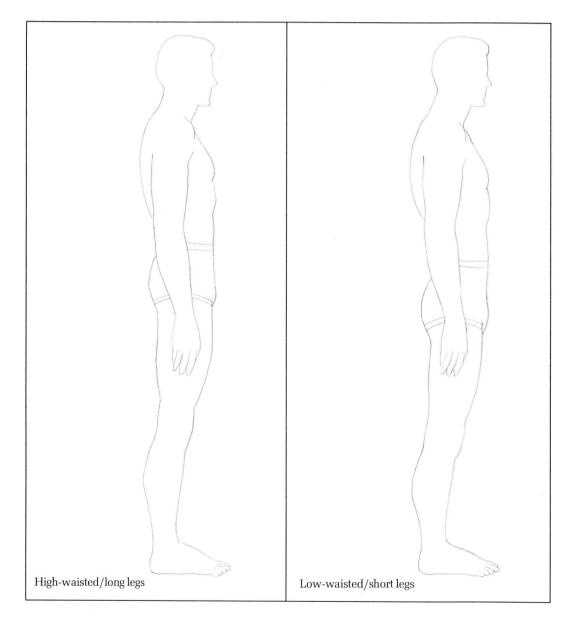

High-waisted/long legs

Low-waisted/short legs

Neck   See if your neck is very short or very long. Anything in between is not a problem. If you have a double chin, or if your chin or jowls rest against your collar, you need to compensate for your short neck. You can also camouflage a very long neck by making small adjustments in collar fit (see Chapter 9, "Your Shirt").

Arms   Your arms are of average length if when they hang loosely at your sides, the bottom knuckle of your fist is parallel to your crotch. Check also to see if one arm is longer than the other.

Upper Back   Stand sideways to the mirror and check the profile of your shoulders and upper back. Is your posture relatively straight, or is your upper back rounded with your shoulders tilted forward?

Seat   While standing sideways to the mirror, check the profile of your seat. Especially flat or prominent buttocks require special attention.

SOLUTIONS

Now that you know which areas of your body require special consideration, it's time to focus on the clothing lines and details that will bring your total look in balance. Some of this information will be covered in greater detail later in this book, but here's an introduction to how to achieve a perfectly balanced look for your body.

Height/Weight

If you want to look taller, add vertical lines. Consider a three-button suit made of solid or pinstriped material rather than plaid or tweed fabric, which tends to add width. In casual wear, you are best in a monochromatic look—perhaps navy pants with navy sweater. A sport coat, sweater, or shirt that contrasts sharply with your trousers will simply cut you in half. Corduroy, with its vertical ribs, is a good choice in casual pants. To continue an unbroken line to the floor, wear your pants uncuffed with only the slightest break in the pant leg, and match or at least blend shoe and trouser color.

If you are too thin, you can look heavier with clothes that add bulk and make use of horizontal lines. Create width in suits by adding some padding to the shoulders and by choosing tweeds and plaids. Avoid three-button suits and coats with heavy waist suppression, which are slimming. If the look suits you, consider wearing widely spaced double rear vents and a double-breasted coat. Rugby shirts and sweaters with horizontal stripes are excellent choices for leisure wear. You are the lucky individual who can wear layers of clothing. Try a polo shirt or turtleneck under your regular sport shirt.

If you want to minimize your height, horizontal lines can divide the length of your body into segments and make you appear shorter. A dark sport coat or sweater with lighter pants is an excellent way to make yourself look shorter. In suits and sport coats, patterns such as glen plaids are better than solids. Pants with cuffs and prominent breaks can also remove inches. Consider wide belts and large buckles or colorful cloth belts with casual wear to provide a strong horizontal line.

To appear slimmer, choose vertical lines that lengthen and narrow your body. Suits with vertical stripes or in solid fabrics are excellent choices. Avoid wide double-breasted suits as well as those with natural shoulders and no waist suppression. (A double-breasted suit with buttons placed closer together can be slimming.) A crisp shoulder line and vertical darts in your suits will remove a few pounds. Heavy tweeds and bulky handmade sweaters will add pounds, but trim sweaters with set-in sleeves and V necks will make you look slimmer.

Shoulder/Hip Proportion

If your shoulders are too broad for your hips, you need to add dimension below the waist. Suit coats with pocket flaps and casual jackets with patch pockets will add needed width. Avoid peaked and extremely wide lapels, which tend to emphasize shoulder width. When selecting pants, look for pleats, on-seam pockets, and bulky or heavy fabrics. Trim sweaters with raglan sleeves will also reduce apparent shoulder width and help create a more balanced look in casual wear. Avoid boat-neck pullovers, as this wide, shallow neckline increases apparent shoulder width.

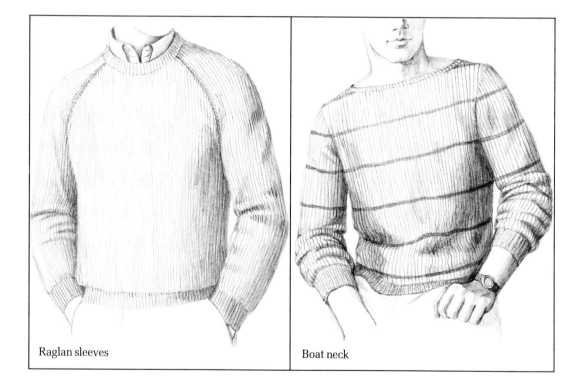

Raglan sleeves   Boat neck

If you have hips that are equal to or wider than your shoulders, emphasize the shoulder and chest area. Add some padding to the shoulders of your suits. When possible, select lapels that point upward and outward. Avoid pants with pleats and on-seam pockets; slant pockets produce a trimmer look. To add width to the shoulders, wear sweaters and shirts with set-in sleeves, and fit them so that the shoulder seams extend slightly beyond your natural shoulder. In casual wear, draw attention upward by combining brightly colored shirts and sweaters with dark slacks. Sweaters and knit shirts with horizontal stripes across the chest and shoulders are ideal.

Shoulder Slope

If your shoulders are tapered, you can make them appear more squarish by slightly padding suit shoulders and by choosing, when possible, lapels that point upward. In sweaters and knit shirts, set-in rather than raglan sleeves will add definition to your shoulders.

Soften the angles of very square shoulders by avoiding padding. Suits and sport coats with natural shoulders are excellent choices. Extremes of lapel width— either wide or narrow—tend to emphasize the shoulder area and call attention to shoulder shape. Lapels or shirt collars that point somewhat downward will also divert attention away from very square shoulders. In sweaters and knit shirts, raglan sleeves and V necks may help to create the illusion of a more tapered shoulder line.

Leg/Torso Proportion

To visually shorten extra-long legs, wear pants with cuffs and a prominent break. Wearing a slightly longer suit jacket and selecting slacks with a lower rise (the distance from crotch to waistband) may also help diminish apparent leg length. Two-button or single-button jackets offer your best proportions in suits or sport coats. Wear your belts as low as possible, and choose contrasting colors for your shirts and pants.

If your legs are short, you can add length by avoiding cuffs and by hemming pants at a length that produces only a slight break in the pants leg over the shoe. Wearing the crotch of your pants as high as is comfortable and shortening your suit jackets slightly will also help create the illusion of longer legs. A three-button suit adds apparent length to your legs as well.

Cuffed pants "shorten" legs while pants without cuffs make legs appear longer.

Waist/Body Proportion

A *high waist* can be camouflaged by pants with a low rise, because the belt will sit low on your waist. Sweaters worn over pants, and slightly longer suit jackets will also help create the illusion of a lower waistline. However, pleated pants should be avoided, as they draw unwanted attention to a high waistline. Casual belts that match or blend with shirt color lengthen the upper body.

A *low waist* can be made to appear higher by wearing pants that have a high rise. Be careful not to make the rise too high, however, as this is not a masculine look. Wide waistbands and belts that match trousers in color can also visually raise the waist. Wearing knit shirts or perhaps even sweaters tucked into the waistband of the pants will also raise the midline. (See illustration on p. 118)

Neck

To disguise a long neck, a good tailor can raise jacket collars. Look for shirt collars that fit high on the neck. Many button-downs fall into this category. Crewneck sweaters and turtleneck shirts are good choices for your casual wardrobe. Avoid open V necks.

A *short neck* will appear longer when you wear V-neck sweaters and open collared shirts. In dress shirts, choose styles with low fitting collars, or have your collars lowered by a tailor. Suits and topcoats will also have to be specially altered to lower the collar. Avoid crewnecks and turtlenecks.

Arms

If you have short arms, lengthen suit-jacket sleeves slightly so that a bit less than the usual half inch of shirt cuff shows. Also, reduce the distance between the hem of the sleeves and the bottom of the jacket by shortening the jacket hem about a quarter of an inch. Suits and sport coats cut with high armholes and raised padded shoulders visually lengthen arms. Sweaters and knit shirts with raglan sleeves may also lengthen arms by providing an unbroken line from collar to cuff.

If you have long arms, allow a bit more shirt cuff to show than the usual half inch. Any cuff visually shortens your arm. Lengthen your jacket a quarter to a half inch. Elbow patches on sportswear may also help to break up a long arm line. In casual wear, rugby shirts and sweaters with stripes on the upper arms help to create balance.

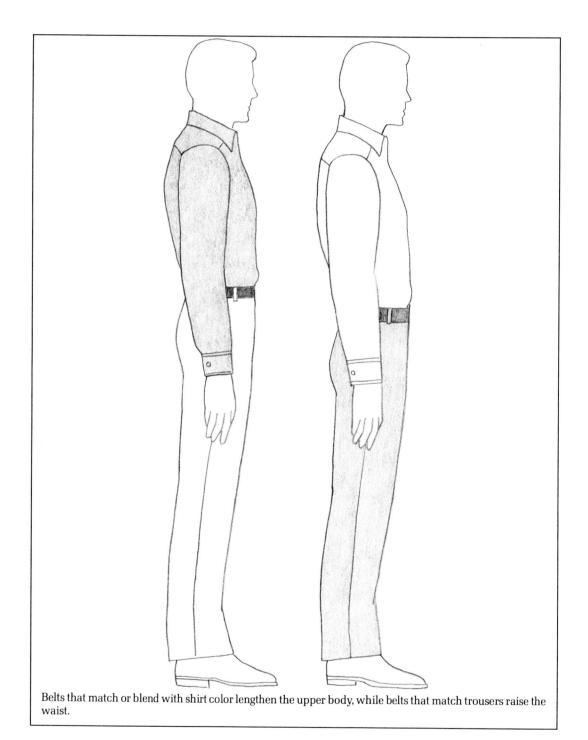

Belts that match or blend with shirt color lengthen the upper body, while belts that match trousers raise the waist.

Upper Back

With a rounded back, you do best to select suits in solid colors, since tailoring the jacket to fit your back often distorts the fabric's pattern at the center back seam, accentuating the roundness. (Pinstripes that have been bowed into a barrel shape greatly emphasize a round back.) Sweaters with horizontal stripes help to camouflage your posture, but collarless shirts make it appear more pronounced.

Seat

If you have a prominent seat, compensate by selecting suit jackets with a single center vent. If you need a high vent to provide extra room, make sure it lies flat. Wearing sweaters out over your trousers will create a smooth line from shoulder to seat. Be careful not to let your sweater ride up in the back, making you look swaybacked.

If your seat is flat, wear jackets with moderate waist suppression and double vents. Trousers must fit flawlessly in the rise (front and back) to avoid a droopy look. For casual pants, corduroys and chinos are better than tight jeans.

A proportioned, finished appearance is vital if you are to stride comfortably and confidently through your business day. Now that you know your own body proportions and how to work with them to create a well-balanced look, let's examine in detail the next essential aspect of being a well-dressed man: the expertly fitted suit.

8

YOUR SUIT: SIZE, CUT, FIT, AND QUALITY

I asked a married couple I know what each would do if given only five hundred dollars to shop for an entire season's wardrobe. The wife admitted she would select several blouses, skirts, and dresses to have a choice of things to wear, even if she had to compromise on quality to do so. The husband said he would buy *one good suit* and wear it every day if necessary.

For most men a suit represents a major investment. A quality suit makes a strong statement about you—your lifestyle, personal credibility, career goals. Choosing a suit in your seasonal palette is only half the mission. In addition, the suit must fit properly.

Clothes can't make the man unless they fit the man! As we've learned, some men are broad-shouldered and narrow-hipped, others have a long line that doesn't vary much from head to toe, while others are long-legged, high-waisted, or square-shouldered. Depending on your build, you'll need a suit cut to fit your body type in order to be well dressed.

Understanding how to fit your body is not difficult. After reading this chapter, you'll be able to guide salesmen and tailors, telling them how you want your suit fitted, and why.

DETERMINING YOUR SUIT SIZE

Ready-to-wear suits come in chest sizes 36 to 50 with pant waists sized six or seven inches smaller. A size 40 suit will come with size 33 or 34 pants, for example. Suits are also sized in short, regular, long, and extra long.

When shopping for a suit, have the salesperson determine your jacket size by measuring around your chest at its widest point (usually under your armpits). This measurement tells you your jacket size. If your arms are heavy or muscular and out of proportion to your chest, you will probably need to buy a bigger size.

Next, measure your waist—over a shirt, but not over trousers—at the point where you normally wear a belt, usually one or two inches below your natural waist. In determining your suit size, always fit the jacket *first*, for it is easier and less expensive to alter pants and vests than it is to adjust a jacket.

Recheck your size each year. Don't keep asking for the same size out of habit. As you gain or lose weight or grow older and gravity takes its toll, your suit size will change.

Figuring out whether you need a short, a regular, or a long takes a bit of care. Generally, shorts fit men who are under 5 feet 8 inches, regulars are for men 5 feet 8 inches to 6 feet, longs are for men 6 feet to 6 feet 4 inches, and extra longs are for men taller than 6 feet 4 inches. Shorts, regulars, longs, and extra longs vary in every dimension, including jacket length, sleeve length, vest length, and rise.

Your height is not the only factor to consider when deciding whether you need a short, regular, long, or extra long. Arm length and the relationship between torso and leg length are just as important. A man who is 5 feet 7 inches may need a regular suit if his torso and arms are long. Men on the borderline between two sizes need to try on several suits and compare fit according to the principles presented later in this chapter.

DETERMINING WHICH CUT IS BEST FOR YOU

Size is one factor and cut is another. There are three basic cuts of suits, and in order to get the best fit, you should match the cut of the suit to your body build.

The Ivy League Suit

This style, made famous by Brooks Brothers, is also known as the sack suit. It has no darts (extra vertical seams) to give shape to the jacket, but rather has a natural, untapered waistline. The chest width is only four to six inches greater than the waist. The jacket has un-padded shoulders, loosely fitted armholes, and a single vent in back. The trousers are fairly full and straight, with only a one-inch reduction in circumference from knee to ankle.

The Ivy League suit is best for the man who has a sturdy build, whether he's large, athletic, or simply on the portly side.

The Updated American Suit

This cut is becoming the most popular style. Unlike the traditional Ivy League suit, the updated American suit has a slightly suppressed waist with added vertical seams in the jacket to give shape and style. The lightly padded shoulders and crisper line are flattering to many body types. This cut also has a higher armhole and smaller waistline in proportion to the shoulders. The drop from chest to waist is six to seven inches. It may have a single or double vent. Like the Ivy League cut, the pants hang straight from the knee, though the circumference of the pants legs is usually smaller than that of Ivy League cut trousers.

The updated American suit is best for the slimmer man. Portly or highly muscular thick men can't fit into this style comfortably.

The European Suit

A high-fashion look, with a seven-inch drop from chest width to waist width, this suit is appropriate for slender men who work in creative professions. This is not a broker's suit! However, the squared shoulders, high armholes, double-vented jacket, and tapered pants do have elegance.

Ask the salesperson how the suits in his store are cut, and don't waste your time trying on styles that are inappropriate for you. At Brooks Brothers, my broad-shouldered, narrow-hipped client found that he could not fit into any of their suits, even their slimmer ones. The salesperson was kind enough to refer him to another store where suits are cut in an updated American style. Perfect!

FIT

Now that you know your size and have determined the cut which best fits your build and lifestyle, you need to have your suit carefully fitted. Every good men's clothier has a professional tailor, though you may prefer to use one who runs his own shop. Knowing exactly how your suit should fit is the key to communicating effectively with the tailor.

Start out by dressing appropriately when you are shopping for a suit or having one fitted. Wear a suit so you will have on a shirt, a tie, and the proper shoes when trying on the new suit. Add all the usual things you carry in your pockets so the tailor can judge the fit correctly.

Jacket

■ Shoulders   The shoulders of a jacket are crucial to a good fit. Check this area first to determine if the proper suit size has been chosen. The seam that joins the sleeve to the jacket should rest at the natural edge of your shoulder, neither hanging over nor being stretched by your arms. (If you have very large arms you may have to have your suits custom-made.)

Before they will reset sleeves to adjust shoulder width, tailors generally recommend trying another jacket size and making other adjustments. Don't be surprised if you have to try on several suits. Another size or a suit from a different manufacturer may make a great deal of difference. If your shoulders are tapered, causing the jacket to bunch due to excess fabric, you can add shoulder pads to correct the problem. The pads will not only improve the fit of the jacket but will give your shoulders a more attractive line as well.

■ Chest   To check for proper chest fit, reach forward to determine if you can move freely. Look at the fabric between your shoulder blades and make sure it does not pull or wrinkle. Small adjustments can be made by taking in or letting out the center back seam of the jacket. If the wrinkles tend to be diagonal, you probably have one shoulder higher than the other. Have a small pad built into the lower shoulder.

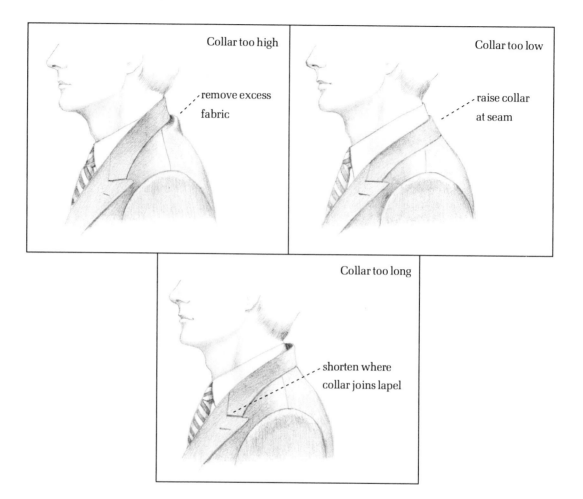

Collar too high — remove excess fabric

Collar too low — raise collar at seam

Collar too long — shorten where collar joins lapel

■ Collar

Very few men can buy a suit without having the collar *raised*, *lowered*, or *shortened*. Square or very tapered shoulders; a neck that is thin or thick, short or long; and a rounded back all create special problems in collar fit.

Look in a three-way mirror. The jacket collar should hug the back of the neck with a half inch of shirt collar showing above it. If the shirt is hidden or there is a buckle of excess jacket fabric just below the suit collar, you need to have the collar lowered. This is done by removing excess fabric from the back of the jacket just under the collar.

If more than a half inch of the shirt collar is showing, the collar should be raised. Extra fabric is built into the collar in all better men's suits.

If the suit collar pulls away from your neck, or if the jacket lapels pull out or buckle, you need to take up the slack by shortening the collar. The collar is shortened at the notch where it joins the lapel in front.

■ Length
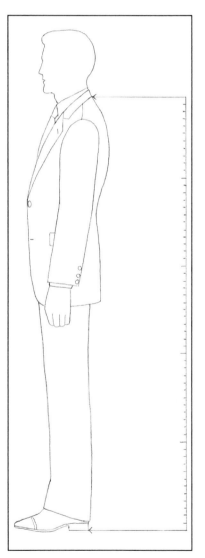
The proper length of a jacket is strictly a matter of proportion. An old rule of thumb was to stand with your arms at your sides, fingers curled under. If the hem of the jacket fell in the curve of the fingers, it was the right length. But this rule does not accommodate people with long or short arms, and you may end up looking unbalanced. Generally, your jacket should be long enough to cover your buttocks. If you have very long legs, however, you may want to wear your jacket slightly longer than your buttocks to make your legs appear shorter and more balanced. If your legs are very short, you'll want to wear your jacket just above the bottom of your buttocks in order to give the illusion of longer legs. Have the tailor measure you (with shoes on) from the lower edge of the suit collar to the floor, and divide the measure-

ment in half. For a well-proportioned look, the bottom of your jacket in back should fall approximately at that halfway point.

Jacket length should be even all around. Unbutton the jacket and check the bottom of the jacket closure. If the sides don't match evenly, you probably have one shoulder lower than the other. Build a pad into the lower shoulder instead of altering the jacket hem. Also, stand sideways in front of a mirror and compare the length of the jacket front and back. If you have rounded shoulders, you may need to lengthen the back of the jacket or shorten the front.

■ Vents   Jacket vents are basted shut by the manufacturer. If necessary, open them to check fit. Button the jacket and check to see if the vent pulls open in back. If it does, you need additional room in the waist and in the lower part of the jacket (the skirt). Have the side seams let out or the buttons moved, or try a combination of both.

■ Torso   If you have excess material in the waist and hip area of the jacket, have the tailor take in the side seams and the back center seam, or all three. If the waist is too tight or appears too suppressed for your taste, have the seams let out.

■ Sleeves   As a general rule, the hem of your sleeve should end just at the break of your wrist, covering your wrist bone, but leaving room to allow a quarter to a half inch of shirt cuff to show. Make sure the tailor checks both sleeves. Most of us have one arm slightly longer than the other. Also, have the tailor check that the fabric in the upper portion of your sleeve isn't too snug or baggy. Sleeves should rest lightly on the upper arms without binding, and should hang smoothly to the bottom when your arms are at your sides. If a sleeve has a diagonal wrinkle in the upper arm, your tailor will have to reset the sleeve and rotate it slightly. This alteration is expensive, and many tailors don't want to do it. If your tailor won't make this change, don't buy the suit. It will never look right.

Vest

Vests are fitted and are always worn with the bottom button open. A vest must cover the waistband of your trousers. If it is too long, have it shortened at the shoulder seams. This alteration raises the armholes, so check for comfort under your arms. If the vest is too short, you probably need to choose a long or extra-long suit. When your suit coat is buttoned, most vests show a little above the jacket's closed lapels. A vest should fit snugly but not so tightly that the buttons pull or strain. Be careful of vests with adjustable tabs on the sides. They often bunch in the back and pull across the front. You will get a smoother fit with a properly tailored vest.

Pants

Try on pants with a belt or suspenders, and put your wallet in your back pocket if you normally carry it there. Check the fit in a three-way mirror so that you can see without twisting and throwing off the natural drape of the fabric. Complete all adjustments to waist, seat, and thigh before marking length.

■ Waist Determine proper waist size by having the tailor pin excess material in back or, if your pants are too small, by unbuttoning the waistband. Before marking the waist size, be sure that the pants are resting where you want them on your hips.

If your hips and waist are close to the same measurement, your slacks may slip down all day, affecting the length. Wearing suspenders will alleviate the problem, and you'll be surprised at how much more comfortable you are.

If your waist is nine inches smaller than your jacket size, you'll need to have your suits custom-made or get a semi-custom suit. You cannot successfully alter pants with that much drop from shoulder to waist with just a nip and tuck. Some stores will totally remake the pants for you, completely take them apart and recut them, which is still cheaper than a custom-made suit. Semi-custom suits, offered by some stores, are similar to off the rack but are made for you according to your measurements—often a very good buy if you have proportion problems.

■ Seat   Check seat fit by looking for wrinkling and sagging in the back (too large) or pulling, especially at the pockets (too small). Major adjustments in the seat generally require an accompanying alteration of the thighs. Always sit in trousers to check the fit; pulling may not be apparent until you are seated. While standing, try swinging your leg forward or taking a few steps. Binding at the knee is another indication that additional room is needed in the seat.

     If the trousers don't rest evenly on your hipbones or if there are diagonal wrinkles at the crotch and thigh area, you probably have one hip higher than the other. An expert tailor may be able to reset the waistband to alleviate the problem.

■ Rise   If the pants extend above your waist or don't come up high enough, the rise is not right for you. Be sure that you have selected the correct suit size in terms of short, regular, or long. A pants waist that is too low cannot be raised, and lowering the waist all around is an expensive alteration. A custom-tailored suit may be the best option in extreme cases.

■ Legs   Turn sideways and look at the way the pants hang. Legs should fall straight and center evenly over each foot. Large calves will cause the pant leg to pull back toward the heel. If you have prominent thighs, the fabric will bind over them when you bend or sit. Only limited alterations are possible in the thigh and calf areas. If this is a problem for you, you may need to reconsider the style of the suit you've chosen. Ivy League suits often have trousers with fuller legs than European or updated American cuts.

     While standing, look down at each pants crease. Ideally the crease should fall centered over the middle toe. If you have bowed legs, the crease will fall over your little toe; if you are knock-kneed, the crease will fall over your big toe. Re-pressing the crease is not the answer to this problem, but adjusting the side seams may accommodate you.

■ Length Alterations to the waist, seat, thigh, and calf areas affect the way pants hang and thus change the overall length. Have the tailor complete all other adjustments before marking length. If alterations to waist, seat, thigh, or whatever involve taking in material, pants may be pinned to approximate the finished product, enabling the tailor to determine the proper length at the first fitting. If seams have to be let out, it is best to have the length marked at the second fitting.

You must wear proper shoes to have the length of trousers marked. The hem of the pants legs should clear the shoe heel and should rest on the front of the shoe with a slight break. The hem may be tapered so that the back hangs slightly longer than the front. Make sure that the tailor measures both legs, since one hip may be higher or one leg longer than the other.

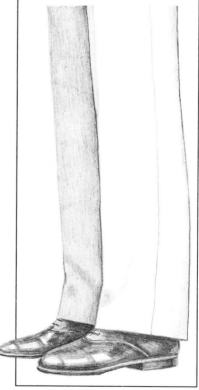

Whether you finish trousers with cuffs or plain bottoms is largely a matter of personal taste and of your desire to make your legs look longer or shorter. If you tend to wear out the back edge of your pants cuff, you can have the tailor sew in a heel stay (an extra layer of fabric) to extend the life of your pants.

QUALITY OF SUIT CONSTRUCTION

The price of a suit depends partly on the amount of time that goes into its construction. Less expensive suits will reflect laborsaving shortcuts. But even an expensive suit, while it may use first-class fabric, may occasionally cut corners on construction to keep the price down.

How do you recognize quality in a man's suit and avoid paying a premium price for a not-so-premium garment? Here are a few points to check when considering a suit.

- ■ Pattern   Check the side and back seams and make sure the patterns match. It requires handwork and more material to make the seams line up correctly. Lower-quality suits may skimp here.

- ■ Sleeve   The buttons on the sleeve should be placed so the edges just touch each other. The buttons should be bone, not plastic, and should be sewn on by hand. A very expensive suit should have buttonholes that really work. Working buttonholes are rarely found on inexpensive garments.

- ■ Collar   Look at the stitching on the underside of the collar. Hand-sewn collars will be flat and hug the neck better. Look for close hand stitching.

- ■ Chest   The material that covers the chest (not including the lapel) has an inner lining to help the garment hold its shape. This interfacing should be sewn in rather than glued or fused. Squeeze the material over the chest and see if it is soft and resilient. If it's stiff, don't buy it.

■ Lining   Some jackets are fully lined, while others have lining only in the front and the top half of the back. Properly lined jackets have an expansion fold on the inside of the hem. The lining should be folded under, neatly pressed, and sewn about a half inch higher than the fold. If the fold is merely rolled under and not properly pressed, the lining will begin to droop and show beneath the hem. When the back of the jacket is lined only at the top, check to be sure that the inside edge of the vent has a small strip of lining sewn in to prevent the flap from curling or riding up.

FABRIC

Choose quality fabric. For the ideal in appearance, fit, and wear, choose a natural fiber, usually wool. You may want to have a small percentage of polyester blended with the wool, as polyester gives the cloth stamina and prevents wrinkles. Natural fibers, especially soft wools or linen, don't hold their shape well except in heavier weights or in sport coats. *Never* buy a double-knit or all-polyester suit. Both look inexpensive and unsophisticated.

A suit in your color made of quality fabric and fitted to perfection is essential to creating an image that brings out your best. Now let's complete the picture with shirts and ties that are just right for you, too.

SUIT MANUFACTURERS

To help you shop, here is a list of manufacturers and the cut and style of their suits.

Name of Manufacturer	Name of Line	Style/Fit (drop)
Bidermann Industries USA, Inc.	Y.S.L.	European (7″)
Brooks Brothers	Brooks Brothers*	Ivy League (5″)
Brooks Brothers	346*	Ivy League (6″)
Brooks Brothers	Brooksgate*	Updated American (7″)
Giorgio Armani	Giorgio Armani	European (7″)
Grief	Chaps	Updated American (7″)
Hart, Marx	Hart, Schaffner, Marx	Updated American (6″) (5″ drop above 42)
Hart, Marx	Hickey Freeman*	Updated American (6″)
Intercontinental Apparel, Inc.	Pierre Cardin	European (7″)
Palm Beach	Haspel	Updated American (6″)
Palm Beach	Palm Beach	Updated American (6″)
Palm Beach	Palm Beach Signature	Updated American (7″)
Phillips, Van Heusen	Cricketeer	Updated American (6″)
Pincus Brothers	Bill Blass	Updated American (6″)
Southwick	Southwick*	Updated American (6″)
Stanley Blacker	Stanley Blacker	Updated American (6″)

* *Available primarily through specialty stores. All others are available through department and specialty stores.*

9

YOUR SHIRT

Your shirt, whether casual or dressy, is the most important item of clothing you wear because it is the color closest to your face. In sportswear, your shirt may set the tone for your whole look. In business and dress shirts, you also have a tie and suit to work with, but your shirt is still the main body of color close to your face.

Don't cheat on color. I learned the downfall of cheating the hard way. One distinguished client was particularly difficult to analyze. He tested well in Summer's powder blue and Winter's icy blue. After considerable testing and even a trip to the store to try on polo shirts and see him in action, I determined he was a Winter. Because of his blue eyes, his gray hair, and the fact that he tested well in Summer's blue, I told him he could cheat a little on his blue dress shirts. I then invited him to attend our annual convention to be an example of a hard-to-analyze client. When he arrived, I almost fell off my platform. My Winter example was wearing a golden tan suit, an ivory shirt, and a blue, red, and tan tie. "Why are you wearing Spring colors?" I asked, aghast. "You told me I could cheat," he said. He looked terrible. I then turned to the two hundred consultants and announced, "We have a new motto. Never tell a client he can cheat a little."

In sportswear, there's no excuse not to look good. You can always find a color that flatters from the wide offering of sport shirts now available. In dress shirts, it may be more difficult to find a specific color, depending on your season. Look quickly through the store, and if it doesn't carry your color, move on. Another store, another buyer, another designer, another manufacturer may give you what you're looking for. You won't have wasted much time in the first store, so you'll still have the time and money to go elsewhere. Eventually you'll know which brands are best for your season.

Aside from color, here are the most important aspects of buying a shirt:

COLLAR

CUFF

FABRIC

PATTERNS

FIT

THE COLLAR

The most noticeable aspect of a shirt, aside from its color and overall quality, is the collar. The *style* of the collar, in addition to suiting your taste, must also suit the style of your other clothes as well as the occasion. The *shape* and *size* of the collar should be in proportion to your face. And of course the collar must *fit*. I will deal with fit in the last section of this chapter. Right now let's look at style, size, and shape.

Collar Styles

There are five basic collar styles: the button-down collar, the standard collar, the pin collar, the full spread collar, and the round collar.

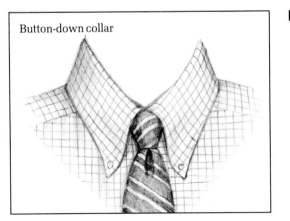

Button-down collar

■ The *button-down collar* is the American favorite. It is appropriate for business, as well as casual and informal social wear. It is not suitable for formal affairs. Button-downs tend to pull and wrinkle when worn with a tie. Make sure that yours are well-fitted, that your tie is not too wide for the collar, and that your shoulders don't pull the shirt fabric, creasing it across the top of your chest and pulling the collar out of line (move the buttons, if need be).

■ *The standard collar* comes in various sizes and shapes with points ranging from short and wide to long and thin. It is dressier than the button-down and suitable for business or social events. The standard collar has crisp, clean lines and looks best when lightly starched and pressed. It is often worn with collar stays, which are removed for laundering.

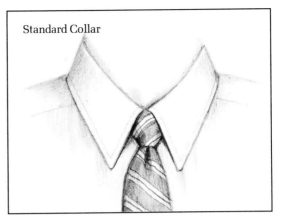

Standard Collar

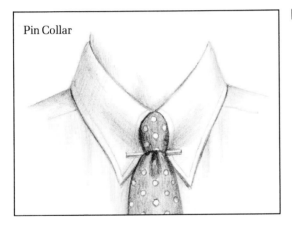

Pin Collar

■ *The pin collar* is a sophisticated, dressy, and more formal collar, usually worn with a three-piece suit. Some collars have holes in them to accommodate the pin or collar bar. You can wear a collar bar on any standard collar as long as it does not have a wide spread. Never pin a button-down.

■ *The full-spread collar* has wide, shortish points that are spread far apart. It is always dressy and European-looking on an American man. It suits those who have a special flair or formality in their personal style. It must be worn with a wide knot in the tie. The full-spread collar does not flatter a man with a wide face.

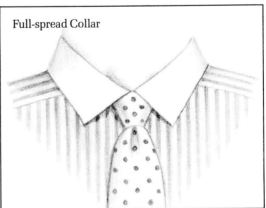

Full-spread Collar

■ *The round collar*, often combined with a collar bar, provides an elegant look. This sophisticated collar is highly favored by the fashion-conscious bankers on Wall Street. It's not a corporate look, so corporate types should reserve it for social wear. It doesn't suit everyone, so don't wear it if you're the rugged, outdoorsy type.

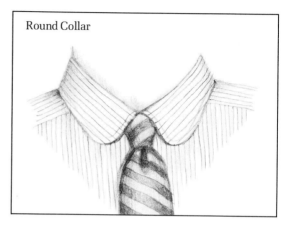
Round Collar

Collar Size and Shape

The *size and shape* of the collar that looks best on you are determined by the size of your head and body and the shape of your face. Ready-made shirts change somewhat from year to year according to fashion. Some styles are faddish and do little for most men. Big strapping American men look pretty silly in the dinky little collars popular in the early eighties. Always flatter yourself rather than compromise your looks to fashion. With subtle adaptations you can be in style and still wear becoming shirts that will last through many a trend.

If you have an oval face or one of average proportions, you can wear most collar styles and need only remember to scale them to your face size and body size. If your face is long and thin or wide and round, you need to be more selective. The variety of collars available in ready-made shirts probably offers enough choice for most men, but some of you will want to invest in custom- or semi-custom-made shirts. These shirts are available mainly through specialty shirt shops rather than stores, but are worth the effort. In a specialty shirt shop you can try on many different collar sizes, shapes, spreads, and even collar heights to see visually what looks best on you. The man with a very short or a very long neck has no choice but a custom shirt. Adjusting the height of your collar will do wonders for the appearance of your neck. Skillfully chosen, your collar can flatter your face and create the illusion of better proportions.

■ *If you have a long, thin face*, choose a collar of medium length that is a little wide. If your shirt is custom-made, choose a spread that is slightly wider than standard. Avoid the very wide European spread, as it is the extreme opposite of your face and will accentuate its thinness.

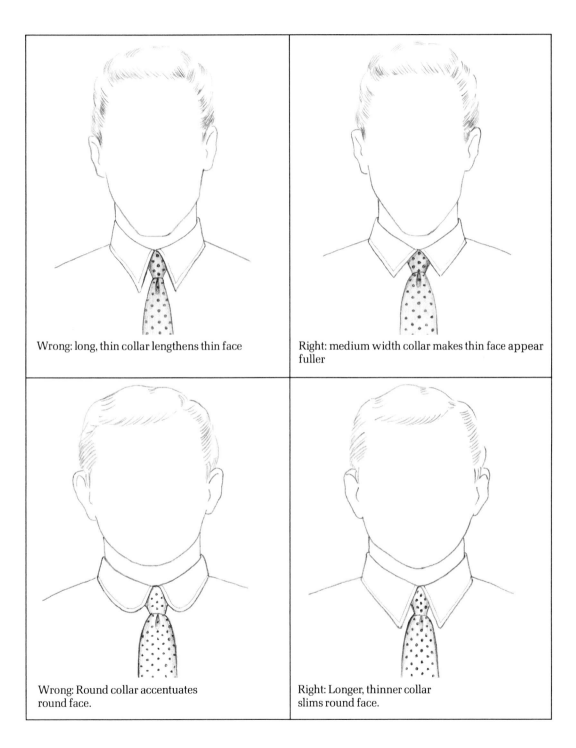

Wrong: long, thin collar lengthens thin face

Right: medium width collar makes thin face appear fuller

Wrong: Round collar accentuates round face.

Right: Longer, thinner collar slims round face.

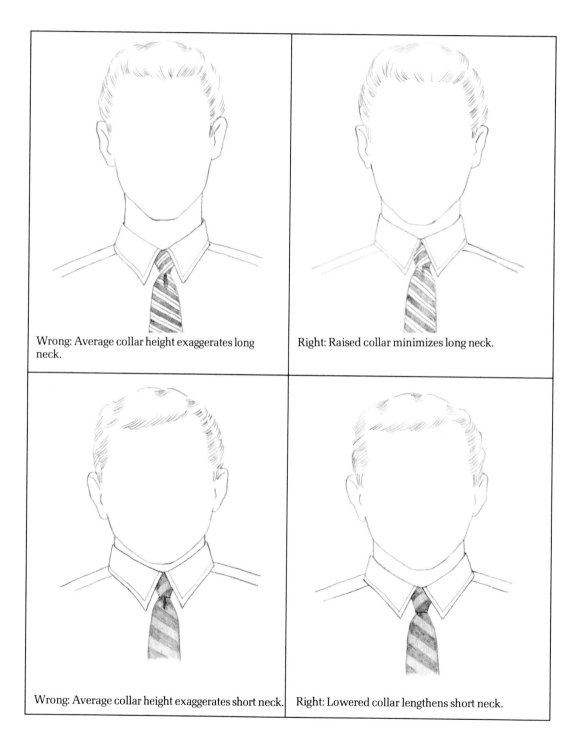

Wrong: Average collar height exaggerates long neck.

Right: Raised collar minimizes long neck.

Wrong: Average collar height exaggerates short neck.

Right: Lowered collar lengthens short neck.

■ *If you have a wide or round face*, it can appear lengthened and slimmed by a slightly longer and thinner collar. An extremely long and thin collar is too out of balance with your face and will accentuate rather than minimize your problem. Avoid round collars, which accentuate roundness, and European spreads, which accentuate wideness.

■ *If you have a long neck*, your collar should be a quarter inch higher all around than the standard cut. Adjust your suit-collar height as well.

■ *If you have a short neck*, choose a shorter collar to keep from looking stubby. Your suit-collar height should be proportionally adjusted, too.

■ *If your neck is wrinkled*, choose a collar higher in front.

■ *If you have a very small or a very large head and face*, your collar size should be scaled to your size: smaller collar for small head, larger for large head. In addition to being in flattering proportion to your face, the collars of your business and dress shirts must be compatible with the style of your suits and sport coats and the shape of your jacket lapels. If you've chosen a slightly wide lapel to suit your face and body shape, don't select a thin, narrow collar. If you're wearing a narrow-lapeled casual jacket, don't accompany it with a European spread shirt collar.

Last, make sure your collars are clean, well-pressed, and not worn out. A collar that is frayed around the edges will blow your image for sure. Shirts that are worn frequently become familiar old buddies. Take a look at yours and toss out the frazzled ones.

THE CUFF

Your cuff is important in creating a finished, well-groomed look. The length of your cuff is critical. Exposed wrists look just as bad as sleeves that are too loose and too long. Cuffs should be a quarter to a half inch longer than your jacket sleeves and should cover the wristbone. Never wear a short-sleeved shirt under a suit. Even in sweltering weather it looks unprofessional.

For the neatest look in a cuff, make sure it fits your wrist trimly. A button on the placket above the cuff is the mark of a fine shirt. This look is found on expensive ready-mades or can be ordered on custom shirts. If you choose French cuffs and cuff links, make sure the formality of this style blends with your suit and is compatible with your personality. French cuffs are usually for dress, but more formal men can wear them for work as well.

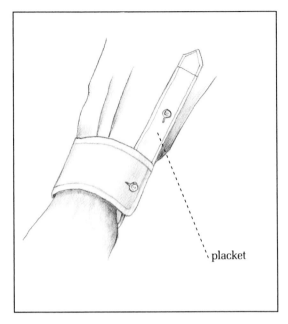

placket

Whatever style of cuff you choose, make sure it is crisply pressed, especially if the fabric is cotton. You can sometimes get away without pressing if your shirt is permanent press, but a stiff, lightly starched cuff gives a more finished look.

THE FABRIC

The best fabrics for dress shirts are 100 percent cotton or cotton/polyester (wash and tumble dry) blends. A shirt of pure cotton looks great, fits, is cool, and takes color well. However, it wrinkles—sometimes badly!—after a day at work. A permanent-press cotton/polyester blend (65 percent cotton/35 percent polyester) may be the best choice for long wear.

The basic choices for business shirt fabrics are broadcloth, oxford cloth, and end-on-end.* In general you will wear like finishes in suits and shirts: broadcloth with worsted (both smooth), oxford with flannel (both slightly textured).

In sport shirts you may choose from cottons, denims, corduroys, flannels, wools, or knits. Take the time to find the right color for you, and select shirts of good quality that will wear well.

Forget 100 percent synthetic fabrics for either business or casual wear. These fabrics almost always look cheap and don't "breathe." Silk shirts are strictly for evening wear or for the flashier professions where it is acceptable to dress up for work. Batiste or any see-through material is not appropriate for business, though in the creative professions it may be acceptable for summer wear.

---

* An end-on-end is a fabric with two colors of thread (say, blue and white) tightly woven together. It is traditionally darker than an oxford cloth.

PATTERNS

Patterns add interest to a shirt but are always less formal than a solid. The rule of thumb is that subtle patterns are suitable for business wear, and noticeable patterns are for casual or social attire. Most men are best advised to stay away from prints of any kind. Pictures, geometric designs, and florals are seldom flattering unless you live in Hawaii, where they are part of the culture.

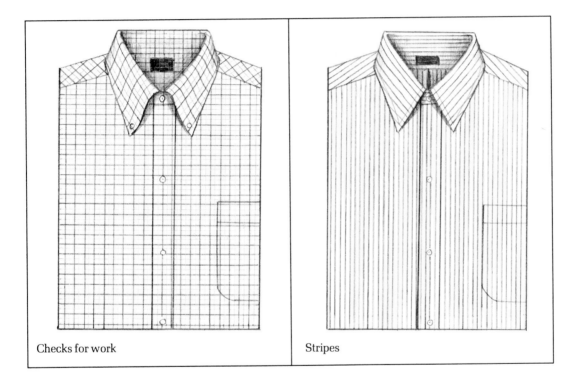

Checks for work

Stripes

Tattersall checks in subtle shades and (particularly in the summer) small, well-defined box checks can be acceptable for some professions. Checks are not a corporate look.

When thin and crisp, stripes go with any style business suit, even a pinstripe. As the stripes get wider or brighter, they become more sporty in appearance.

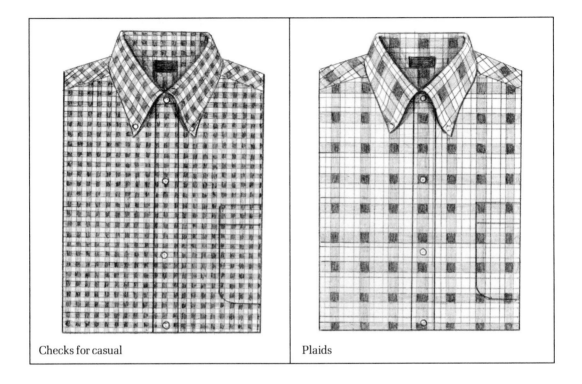

Checks for casual | Plaids

From muted to bold, tattersall to gingham, checked shirts are generally most suitable for sportswear.

Any bright, busy combination of colors is immediately casual, but subtle plaids can be worn with a sportcoat for some professions.

THE FIT

When selecting a ready-made shirt, you have only neck circumference and sleeve length to go by. If your arm length and neck size are not compatible with the standard size, you'll need a custom shirt. In ready-mades you may also have to choose between an ill-fitting torso and an ill-fitting collar, since most manufacturers use a standard proportion of collar size to chest width. If you find yourself in this situation, choose an ill-fitting torso with a well-fitted collar, since the collar is the more visible. Some manufacturers do cut shirts fuller or slimmer, so ask the salesman which brand and designers are best for your build. (When you have your shirts custom-made, the dilemma of proper fit is avoided.)

Many men will have some fit problem with a ready-made shirt, but may find custom-made shirts prohibitively expensive. Although a tailor-made-from-scratch shirt is expensive, the independent shirt shops that specialize in semi-custom shirts offer much more reasonable price ranges. You can try on torso size and taper as well as collar and cuffs. The store measures your neck and arms and guarantees fit. In addition, you can choose your fabric and—hurray!—your colors from a large assortment. These shirts last forever, and you can even have the collar replaced if it wears out. If you have any fitting problems, it's worth the time and expense to get a shirt that does your body justice and in which you feel terrific.

Fitting the Collar

The collar's fit is crucial. If it is too tight, it will pull and wrinkle, so even the finest shirt will look poorly chosen. If the collar is too loose, you will look messy.

To measure your neck properly, measure around the lower part of your neck at the point where the collar button rests. The ends of the tape measure should touch, but the tape should not be pulled tightly. You want to have enough leeway so that a tie, when knotted, will not strangle you.

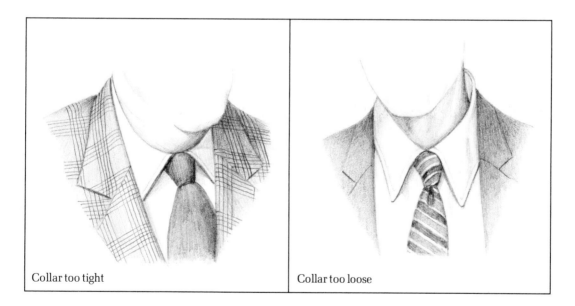

Collar too tight | Collar too loose

If your collar wrinkles when buttoned and worn with a tie, it is probably too tight. If you have square shoulders, your button-downs will wrinkle even if the collar size is correct. You may be able to adjust the buttons by moving them to a point where the collar doesn't pull. If that doesn't work, don't wear button-downs, or have them custom-made so the shoulder can be cut differently.

Recheck your collar size every year or anytime you gain or lose weight. As you age, your neck size will change. My father was a surgeon who was more interested in his patients than his shirts. Year after year he ordered the same size shirts until one morning my mother found him with a razor, slitting the buttonhole on his brand-new shirt collar. "What are you doing?" she cried. "My shirt's too tight," he replied. We wondered how many years he'd been slitting his buttonholes instead of buying bigger shirts.

Fitting the Cuffs and Sleeves

Measure the length of your arm from the center of the nape of your neck along your shoulder and down to your wristbone. A custom shop should measure both arms in case one is longer than the other. In ready-mades, buy the length that fits your long arm and have the other sleeve shortened.

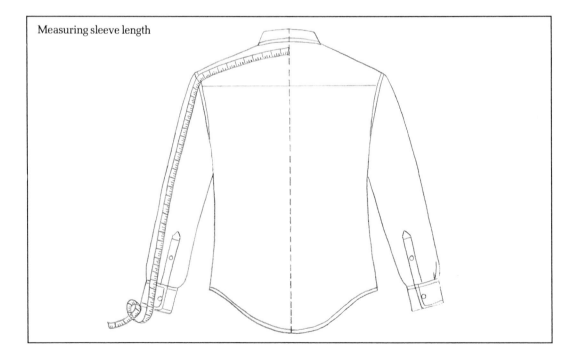

Measuring sleeve length

Your cuff should fit closely around your wrist but still be comfortable. Adjust the buttons if necessary. Some shirts come with two buttons sewn on so you can button whichever fits your wrist best. Remember, cuffs should not extend much more than a half inch below your jacket sleeve. By the same token, never settle for a sleeve that is too short.

If your arms are extremely broad or muscular, you may need a custom shirt in order to build more fullness into the sleeve. Skimpy sleeves not only are uncomfortable but will also pull on the shirt yoke and make your collar wrinkle.

Fitting the Shoulders

An ill-fitting shirt that is too tight will pull, creating long creases in the fabric across your collarbones. A shirt too loose in the shoulders will sag across the front. The standard shirt yoke is cut for shoulders that taper two inches from the bottom of the neck to the edge of the shoulder.

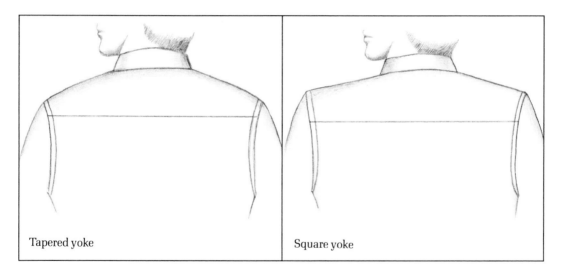

Tapered yoke

Square yoke

- *If you have square shoulders,* you'll need a square yoke or your collars will always pull and wrinkle. Square yokes have to be custom-made, though some fashion designers cut a yoke that is more square than the standard.
- *If your shoulders are quite tapered,* you'll need an extra-tapered yoke—again, custom-made. You may also need your collar shortened.

Fitting the Torso

The taper of the shirt body is a matter of both comfort and looks. You want to avoid any pulling or constriction across your stomach, as well as any bunching up or bagging of surplus fabric. A trim, slightly loose line wears best and is most comfortable. Make sure the shirt is long enough to stay tucked in.

Try on different brands to see which are cut for you. Some designer shirts and European cuts are slimmer through the torso. A tailor can put darts in a shirt that's too full, thus reducing the excess bulk.

Now you know everything you need to know to successfully buy and fit a shirt. When you find a shirt you really like, buy two, so you'll always have your favorite shirt clean and ready to wear.

Invest some time and effort in your shirt wardrobe—both casual and dress. A shirt in some form is one item of clothing you wear every day of your life.

SHIRT MANUFACTURERS

To help you shop here is a list of shirt manufacturers and the cut of their shirts.

Name of Manufacturer	Name of Line	Style/Fit
Alexander Julian	Alexander Julian*	Medium range
Arrow	Arrow	Fitted and medium range
Brooks Brothers	Brooks Brothers*	Full cut
Gitman Brothers	Gitman Brothers*	Medium range
Manhattan	Henry Grethel	Medium range
Manhattan	John Henry	Fitted
Manhattan	Manhattan	Fitted and medium range
Palm Beach	Eagle	Medium range
Palm Beach	Gant	Full cut
Palm Beach	Pierre Cardin	Fitted
Van Heusen	Van Heusen	Fitted and medium range
Warnaco	Chaps	Full cut
Warnaco	Christian Dior	Fitted and full cut
Warnaco	Hathaway	Full cut

* *Available primarily through specialty stores. All others are available through department and specialty stores.*

10

YOUR TIE

Every evening after work Harry frequented a New York bar where it was the custom for a man to loosen his shirt and hang his tie on a peg on one wall. Every night hundreds of ties adorned the wall, signifying the end of a hard day's work. One night Harry—who was a well-dressed and respected fellow—hung up his tie as usual, only to let out a cry, leave the bar, and return a few minutes later with a pair of scissors. Harry took his tie off the peg and ceremoniously cut it to shreds. The bartender said, "My God, man, why are you cutting up an expensive silk tie?" And Harry replied, "Because there is another tie just like mine up there. My tie is the only way I have of expressing my individuality!" And then he ordered a double.

Your tie can make or break your image. When chosen wisely, it brings color to your face, style and class to your dress, and individuality to your business "uniform."

Yet many men shop for a tie as if it were to be worn by their shirt and suit alone. You will often see a man bring the suit and shirt to the counter and start trying the ties on the items of clothing, not thinking to try each tie on himself. I have often demonstrated to my clients how much impact—or how little—a tie has by having them try it on. The salespeople at better men's stores in my town are quite used to seeing men standing in front of a mirror holding shirts and ties under their faces.

Naturally a tie must look good with your suit and shirt, but never at the expense of your face or personality. If possible, buy the suit first, then select the tie, and then choose a shirt to match both. The guidelines for combining coat, shirt, and tie are in Chapter 11.

To buy the best ties for you, consider: PATTERN

COLOR

FABRIC

WIDTH

LENGTH

Let's look at each of these factors.

PATTERN

There are eight basic types of patterns:

1. Solid
2. Rep (Striped)
3. Foulard (Ivy League)
4. Club
5. Plaid
6. Geometric
7. Dots
8. Paisley

Each one of these patterns has a different effect and is appropriate with different styles of suits and jackets. A useful tie wardrobe will include a sampling of patterns so that the look of any suit can be modified, making your clothes as versatile as possible.

Solid

Solids go well with solid suits, patterned jackets, and all shirts. They are versatile, and can be either bold or conservative. Dark silk solid ties have a quiet elegance, while casual wools and knits bring either subtle or bright color to your wardrobe without being busy or loud. Some solids have a same-color pattern—a red-on-red stripe, for example. These are considered solids as long as the pattern is subtle. Silk solids have a sheen that adds richness to the tie, but stay away from very shiny or brocade versions.

Tie Patterns

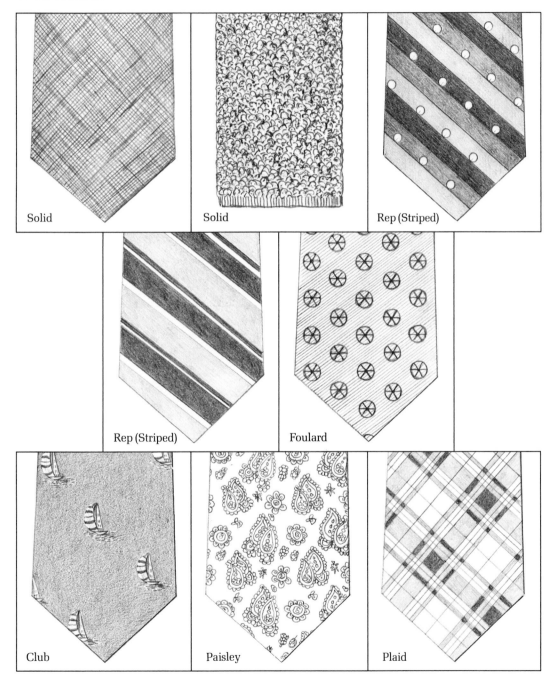

Solid

Solid

Rep (Striped)

Rep (Striped)

Foulard

Club

Paisley

Plaid

Rep (Striped)

Striped ties are based on the old regimental patterns. These days any diagonal stripe is called a rep. This is the classic American business tie. Stripes may be quite thin, of varying widths, or even and wide. Your selection will depend on your body proportions and personality. With clear-colored suits, keep the stripes crisp; with suits in muted tones, the stripes should be softer.

Foulard (*Ivy League*)

The term *foulard* was originally applied to a weave of fabric with a corded appearance. Today it is used for an Ivy League tie pattern made up of a series of small, regularly spaced designs such as circles, ovals, diamonds, or squares on a solid background. A foulard is often quite elegant. The small, subtle pattern brings color to the tie without being loud.

Club

The club tie can be sporty or conservative. It has a regular pattern of club-like motifs—such as heraldic shields, sporting insignia, or animals—against a solid background. The pattern should be small, subtle, and not instantly recognizable. A tie with big, bold figures on it is *not* a club tie, and is generally considered tacky.

Plaid

Plaid ties are usually considered casual. In heavy wool they are appropriate in the wintertime with tweeds and muted herringbone. They do not go with pin-striped suits or the sleeker worsteds. They can go well with flannel suits, however, and when made of linen or cotton, plaid ties go with summer suits as well. Just remember to avoid garish or loud plaids at any time of year.

Geometric

Geometric ties cover everything from an enlarged diamond pattern resembling an Ivy League tie to crisscross or vertically striped patterns. The large diamond shapes are more casual than the smaller versions, but either brings an angularity to your appearance—particularly flattering to the large man.

Dots

Dots range from polka dots to pin dots. Traditionally a very elegant tie, the polka dot is almost as versatile as the solid tie. Very small pin dots are even more formal, and are used for evening or with your more elegant business suits for special occasions.

Paisley

Paisley ties are useful because they combine so many colors that they mix and match well. In stronger colors paisley ties are too sporty for a business look, but when the colors and fabric are subdued, these ties can be elegant and dressy.

COLOR

Your tie color can enhance your face, add zip to your total appearance, and work as an accent to complete your outfit. It can also be a powerful tool for bringing an old wrong-color suit into line. Always wear your right color as the primary color in the tie. Choose a patterned tie with a background color from your chart and a design that brings in a small amount of the wrong color from your suit. The tie will then blend harmoniously with the suit, while its primary color offsets to some degree the suit's negative effect. Once your wardrobe has been changed over completely, however, try to buy only ties with your correct colors. There may be a touch of wrong color in patterned ties, but the more visible the wrong color is, the less it will do you justice.

Following are some guidelines for each season's ties.

Winters

Winters need clear, sharp colors. When shopping for a navy tie, be careful to buy a bright or dark navy rather than a muted one. Winters look excellent in solid colors, since a pattern can diminish the contrast or sharpness of the tie under a Winter's face. Solid dark blue-reds are especially flattering. Any patterns should contain some brightness or contrast. Best prints for the Winter man are stripes with sharp contrast (the width of the stripes depends on your body scale, face size, and personality). Second best are foulard ties, if the tiny repeat patterns contain some element of brightness or contrast. A tiny white diamond, for example, is better than a muted blue diamond. Geometrics are good for Winters. Polka dots are fine as long as they are sharp and suit your personality. Plaids are rarely appropriate for a Winter, since a plaid that offers enough contrast is usually too loud for business wear. Paisleys are similarly problematic, but are occasionally okay if carefully selected. If the paisley is subtle, then you must wear a pure white or a very icy shirt to provide the sharpness your look needs. A club tie is not your most exciting look. Wear it only if you are sentimental about the emblem.

Summers
Summers should choose more subtle ties in shades slightly more muted than Winter's. A Summer's best print is the foulard, especially when the pattern is in a rounded shape such as a teardrop or oval. Summers should wear stripes that offer minimal contrast or look blended (either thin or wide, depending upon body scale, face size, and personality). Plaids are okay as long as they are blended; a subtle madras plaid works well. Dots are fine, too, as long as they are fairly small and not too sharp. Few Summers wear paisleys, but if they suit you, keep the pattern subtle and blended. Clubs are fine if the insignia is not too bright and the motif is conservative.

Autumns
The Autumn man needs richness in the colors of his ties. Often he has no cheek color, and he depends upon that tie to brighten his face. Most Autumns look excellent in patterned ties, especially rich paisleys. Plaids are great as well, particularly in combination with Autumn's tweeds and herringbones. Irregular stripes are also good, though ties with evenly spaced stripes of equal width may be too contrived and controlled for an Autumn man. Polka dots may also be too formal for you. Foulard ties are fine in almost any pattern as long as the scale suits your face and body size. Sporty club ties are good for Autumns.

Springs
Springs, like Winters, depend on clear colors, so their ties should never look dull or washed out. The Spring man wears solids well, usually in ties with a matte (nonshiny) finish. The best prints for Springs are casual, subtle plaids, widish stripes with medium contrast, and almost any foulard pattern. Severe stripes are too sharp for most Spring men, and polka dots are usually too formal. Sporty club motifs are good for Springs. A paisley will work only if it is carefully chosen in your colors. In general, it is not Spring's best look. Most geometrics are too severe for Springs.

WINTER		SUMMER	
Solid	Excellent for contrast. Choose clear, sharp colors, especially in navy or red.	Solid	Good in muted shades, medium to dark.
Rep (Striped)	Excellent. Choose sharply contrasting stripes.	Rep (Striped)	Good with blended stripes, subtle contrast.
Foulard	Select patterns with brightness or contrast.	Foulard	Excellent, especially when pattern is in a rounded shape such as teardrop.
Club	Personal choice. Insignias better than sporty motifs.	Club	Personal choice. Avoid anything too bright.
Plaid	Seldom appropriate.	Plaid	Subtle plaids, such as gentle madras, are good.
Geometric	Excellent.	Geometric	Subtle rather than bold.
Dots	Choose sharp polka dots with high contrast.	Dots	Dots are fine, usually small and not too sharp.
Paisley	Seldom appropriate. Choose sophisticated neutrals rather than bold colors.	Paisley	Seldom appropriate but okay if soft and blended.

AUTUMN		*SPRING*	
Solid	Good in rich colors.	Solid	Good in clear colors, never dull or washed out.
Rep (Striped)	Good in irregular stripe.	Rep (Striped)	Choose medium-contrast stripes.
Foulard	Almost any pattern okay.	Foulard	Almost any pattern okay.
Club	Sporty club motifs are fine.	Club	Sporty club motifs are fine.
Plaid	Excellent, especially with tweeds and herringbone.	Plaid	Excellent in casual, subtle plaids. Gentle madras is good.
Geometric	Probably too formal.	Geometric	Probably too severe.
Dots	Probably too formal.	Dots	Probably too formal.
Paisley	Excellent.	Paisley	Seldom appropriate.

FABRIC

A tie is never as effective—even one in the right color and pattern—if it is made of a cheap fabric. Both the surface and drape of the fabric are important. Silk, fine wool, linen (for summer), and cotton are the best fabrics. Stay away from synthetics if possible. Not only do good fabrics take color better, but they also knot better than cheaper ones.

Generally any matte or flat-finish fabric can be worn for business, dress, or casual occasions. Nubby textures are always more casual. A subtle sheen on silk is elegant in business wear and can be quite fancy. Shiny ties are strictly dress wear, but they must be silk and in a color conservative enough to keep the shine from being overwhelming.

Tie Width

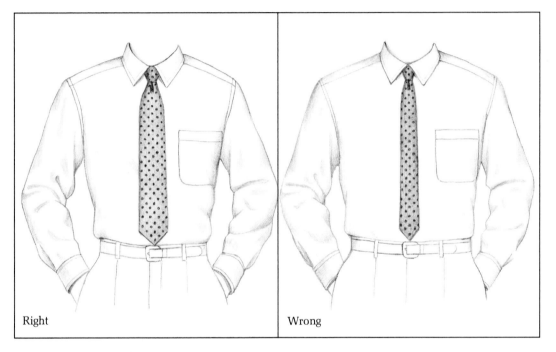

Right

Wrong

The width of ties varies somewhat according to fashion, but the most flattering width for all men is between 3 and 3½ inches at the tie's broadest point. If you are broad-chested, you'll want a broader tie. If you are thin, choose narrower ties.

In addition, you need to have the tie in proportion to your collars. Here, too, it is a subtle difference, not a large one, that bespeaks style and savvy.

Tie Length

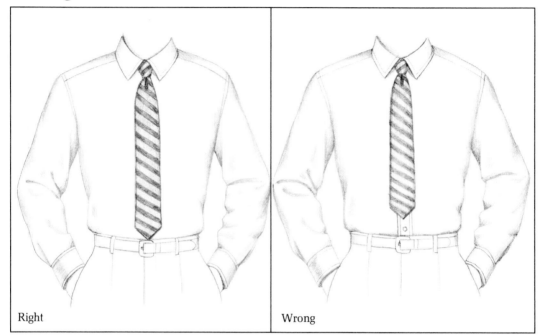

Right

Wrong

The length of your tie should always be the same. When it is tied properly, the tip of your tie should hit just at the top of your belt. You will need to adjust the length when tying it. Depending upon your height you will need more or less fabric to achieve this.

KNOTS AND BOW TIES

How you wear the tie is as important as the tie itself. There are three standard knots; each one is suitable with different shirt collars and your overall body proportions. The tie knot should lie comfortably between your collar points with no gaps on either side and no pinching or crowding. Both wide-faced and thin-faced men should avoid very thin or very wide knots, which accentuate any proportion problems by either repeating the line or offering too extreme a contrast.

The following illustrations are drawn in mirror image, so you can prop the book up facing you while you stand in front of the mirror

The Four-in-Hand

The four-in-hand is a longish knot and is proportioned for the button-down collar or the standard collar of average spread. Because this knot gives a longer finished tie, it is excellent for the tall man who needs a little more length.

1. Place the wide end of the tie on your right so it hangs about 12 inches longer than the narrow end.
2. Wrap the long end around the short end and then behind, finishing on the right.
3. Continue to cross long end over short end, finishing on the left.
4. Pull long end through loop from the back.
5. Slip point through front of knot and tighten.
6. While pulling down short end with one hand, use other hand to slide knot up snugly.

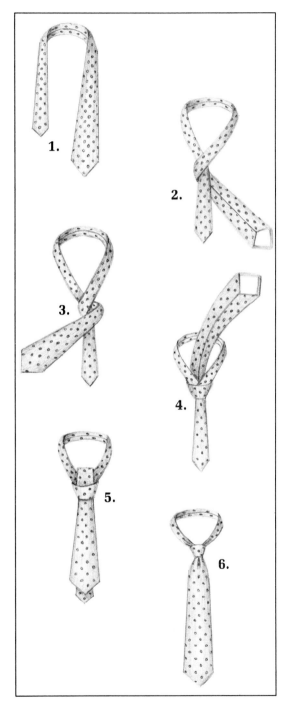

Look at this illustration as if you were looking in a mirror.

The Half Windsor

The half Windsor is more triangular and is also proportioned for the standard collar.

1. Place the wide end of the tie on your right so it hangs about 12 inches longer than the narrow end.
2. Wrap the long end behind the short end, finishing on the right.
3. Thread long end through loop and pull down to the left.
4. Cross long end over knot.
5. Pull long end through loop from the back.
6. Slip point through front of knot and tighten. While pulling down short end with one hand, use other hand to slide knot up snugly.

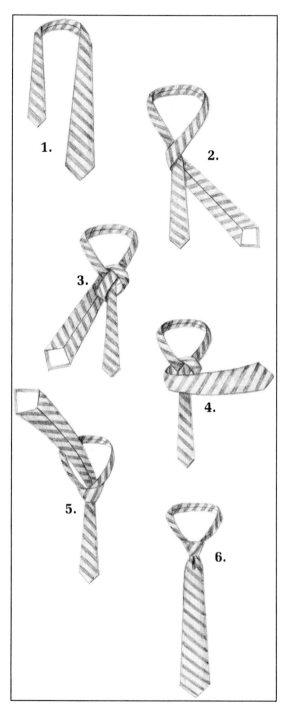

Look at this illustration as if you were looking in a mirror.

The Windsor

The Windsor knot is wide and triangular and is specifically for a European spread or any shirt collar with a widish spread.

1. Place the wide end of the tie on your right so it hangs about 12 inches longer than the narrow end.
2. Cross the long end over the short end and pull up through loop from the back.
3. Bring long end down and wrap behind short end, finishing on the right.
4. Thread long end through loop, then pull down and wrap across front of knot.
5. Thread through loop again.
6. Slip point through front of knot and tighten. While pulling down short end with one hand, use other hand to slide knot up snugly.

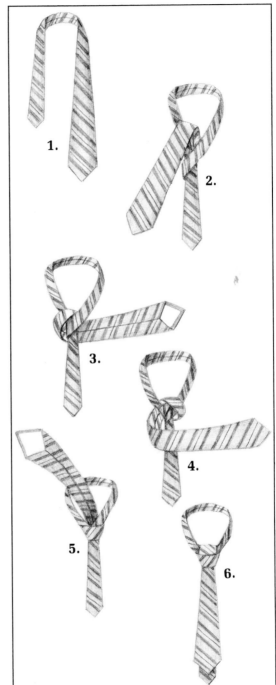

Look at this illustration as if you were looking in a mirror.

The Bow Tie

Wearing the bow tie is a matter of personal choice. But in all but formal attire, it is less serious or businesslike. The same thought and care should be given to the selection of its color, pattern, and fabric as for the standard tie. Avoid clip-ons, even with a tuxedo.

If you are going to wear a bow tie, here's a simple way of making a neat bow:

1. Pull left end to extend 1½ inches below right end.
2. Cross long end over short end and pull up through loop from the back. Pull tight.
3. Fold short end to form front loop of bow.
4. While securing front loop with left hand, pull long end down across loop center.
5. Loop long end around right forefinger toward chest.
6. Push new loop through knot behind first loop. Pull tight and adjust evenly.

Now read on to find out the best ways to successfully put your coat, shirt, and tie together. Although each is important separately, your overall image depends on how well you combine them.

Look at this illustration as if you were looking in a mirror.

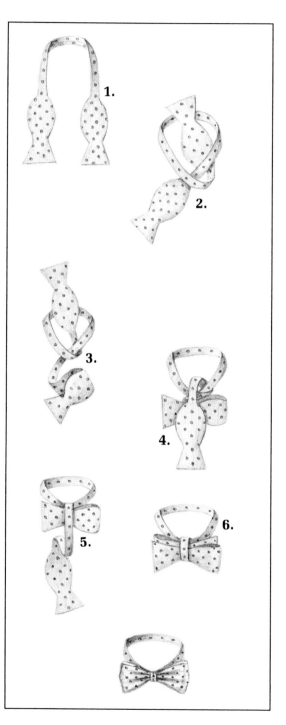

COMBINING COAT, SHIRT, AND TIE

Using your seasonal chart and the guidelines in this chapter you can combine your suits and sport coats with shirts and ties with minimal effort and maximum impact.

The approach to putting your clothes together is always the same. Think of your suit as your basic building block. It establishes the overall color, style, and look you are aiming for. Your shirt can be your white or any light color in your palette that is compatible with the suit and the occasion. Your tie must then relate to the shirt color, the suit color, or both.

With those principles in mind, follow these do's and don'ts to enjoy the pleasure of putting yourself together with grace and impact.

DO: BUY ONLY COLORS FROM YOUR CHART

Buying clothes exclusively in your colors is the secret to successful color combinations. Using the Color for Men system, blending suits or coats with your shirts and ties will be more fun and much easier than ever before. All your clothes will go together because they are in compatible colors of your season and because you will buy shirts and ties that work interchangeably with your suits. If you have suits in the wrong colors, I realize you may have to purchase a few compromise ties until you are able to phase out the suit (and the tie!). But once your wardrobe has completed its transition, don't buy anything *new* in a wrong color.

DO: COMBINE THREE SOLIDS

Wearing a solid-color shirt, suit, and tie is perfectly acceptable and a sure way to look good. This is *not* a boring look if the colors are compatible (which they automatically are, using the Color for Men system) and look terrific on you (which they will). It is low-key, suitable for business, but also elegant. After all, what's more elegant than a tuxedo?

Although all three clothing items are solids, you are actually combining only two colors, or two colors plus one neutral. Here are some rules for combining three solids tastefully and effectively.

■ If your shirt is your season's white, pale gray, or beige (i.e., pale neutral), then your suit and tie may be two distinctly different colors. Usually your tie will be the accent color. In sportswear the same principle applies, as long as the pants are gray, beige/tan, or your white.

Here are examples, by season, of combinations of three solids with a neutral shirt and two distinct colors, using the tie as accent:

Winter: navy suit; white shirt; blue-red tie.
Summer: navy suit; soft white shirt; burgundy tie.
Autumn: navy suit; oyster shirt; rust or bittersweet red tie.
Spring: navy suit; ivory shirt; light rust tie.

■ If your shirt is a color (blue, pink, etc.), then two of the three clothing items must be from the same color family. A color family is a series of tints or shades of the same color. Light blue and navy are both from the blue family. Pink and burgundy are from the blue-red family. Peach and rust are from the orange-red family. Other same-color combinations are beige and brown, buff and golden brown, ivory and camel, gray and black, salmon and tomato red.

Here are examples, by season, of combinations of three solids in which the shirt is a color and the tie is in the same color family as either the shirt or the suit:

Winter: navy suit; icy pink shirt; bright burgundy tie (tie and shirt are same color family).

Summer: blue-gray suit; light blue shirt; navy tie (tie and shirt are same color family).

Autumn: coffee suit; peach shirt; brown tie (tie and suit are same color family).

Spring: tan suit; peach shirt; light rust tie (tie and shirt are same color family).

DO: *COMBINE TWO SOLIDS WITH ONE PATTERN*

The second surefire look is created by combining two solids or semi-solids with one pattern. A semi-solid is a pattern that is so subtle that it gives the appearance of being solid. This can include a suit with a pattern that fades into the overall background or a tweed that is so closely woven with noncontrasting colors that the eye perceives it as solid.

■ *If you choose a patterned tie, it must pick up the suit color, the shirt color, or both colors.*

Your tie must have some reasonable relationship to the color of your suit or your shirt, preferably both. The most common error is choosing a tie that doesn't relate to both items or, sometimes, even to one. For best results, try to pick a tie pattern that repeats the suit color *and* the shirt color. If that's not possible, then repeat at least one. It's okay to have a few extra colors in the pattern as long as the suit and/or shirt colors are there.

In sportswear, your patterned tie may pick up the color of the pants instead of the shirt and/or coat.

Here are examples, by season, of combining two solids with a
patterned tie:

Winter: navy suit; white shirt; navy, red, and white striped tie.
Summer: navy suit; soft white shirt; foulard tie with burgundy
background and navy, soft white, and medium blue
pattern.
Autumn: navy suit; oyster shirt; paisley tie in brown, blue, oyster
white, and beige.
Spring: navy suit; ivory shirt; striped or plaid tie in shades of red,
light blue, navy, and ivory.

■ *If you choose a patterned shirt it must pick up the color family of either the
suit or the tie.*
The solid tie should not be the same color as the solid suit unless it matches
exactly, which is nearly impossible. Unmatching navies are a common error.

Here are examples, by season, of combining two solids with a
patterned shirt:

Winter: navy suit; red tie; dark blue and white hairline-striped
shirt.
Summer: navy suit; red tie; light blue and white oxford-striped shirt.
Autumn: navy suit; bittersweet tie; bittersweet and oyster white
oxford-striped shirt.
Spring: navy suit; rust tie; tattersall check shirt in blue and brown.

■ *If you choose a patterned suit containing threads of color woven into the
background, the tie must pick up a color from the suit.*

■ *If you choose a monochromatic, patterned suit, the solid tie can be a different, contrasting color.*

■ *In sportswear, if you choose a patterned jacket, the same principles apply for the shirt and tie. The solid pants should pick up a color from the jacket.*

Here are examples, by season, of combining two solids with a patterned suit:

Winter: charcoal gray pinstriped suit; white shirt; red tie.
Summer: blue-gray glen plaid suit with subtle burgundy threads; soft white shirt; burgundy tie.
Autumn: brown and beige tweed suit; oyster shirt; bittersweet tie.
Spring: herringbone suit in golden brown, tan, and light beige; ivory shirt; brown or rust tie.

DO: COMBINE ONE SOLID WITH TWO NONCOMPETING PATTERNS

This combination is tricky because it leaves room for error. It's not as sure or easy as combining three solids, or two solids and one pattern. When done correctly, this combination subtly announces that you know your clothing! When wrong, alas, it loudly proclaims the opposite.

If you are unsure of your ability to recognize noncompeting patterns, avoid putting two patterns adjacent to each other and you'll be safer. In other words, your shirt will be solid.

In sportswear, the same principles apply. Whether you choose a patterned coat or patterned pants, your second pattern will probably be your tie. The other two items will be solids.

The basic principles are:

■ *Use a subtle pattern with a stronger one.* Two subtle ones look washed out. Two bold ones are garish. A pinstriped shirt, which is subtle and evenly spaced, looks best if the tie has widish stripes rather than thin, evenly spaced stripes.

■ *Keep the lines of the patterns the same, or use one directional pattern with one all-over pattern.* Because both plaids and stripes have directional lines, they usually don't mix well with each other because the lines compete. However, a subtle stripe can mix with a bolder stripe or a subtle checked shirt can mix with a plaid tie because the lines are similar. Foulard, paisley, and club ties are all-over patterns, as are tweed, herringbone, tiny box checks, or very subtle glen plaids in suits. These patterns can often mix with stripes or plaids. Two all-over patterns can mix as well, as long as one is subtle and the other stronger, or one is large and the other smaller.

Here are examples of combining a patterned suit or coat and tie with a solid shirt:

■ Pinstriped suit; striped, foulard, or dot tie; solid shirt.
■ Chalkstriped suit; heavier pattern in stripes, foulard, or dot tie; solid shirt.
■ Seersucker suit; club, foulard, or soft, wider-striped tie; solid shirt.
■ Subtle business tweed or herringbone suit; striped or foulard tie; solid shirt.
■ Heavy tweed sport coat; wider-striped, ribbed knit, or club tie; solid shirt; solid pants.
■ Wool houndstooth pants; subtle striped or ribbed knit tie; solid shirt; solid coat.

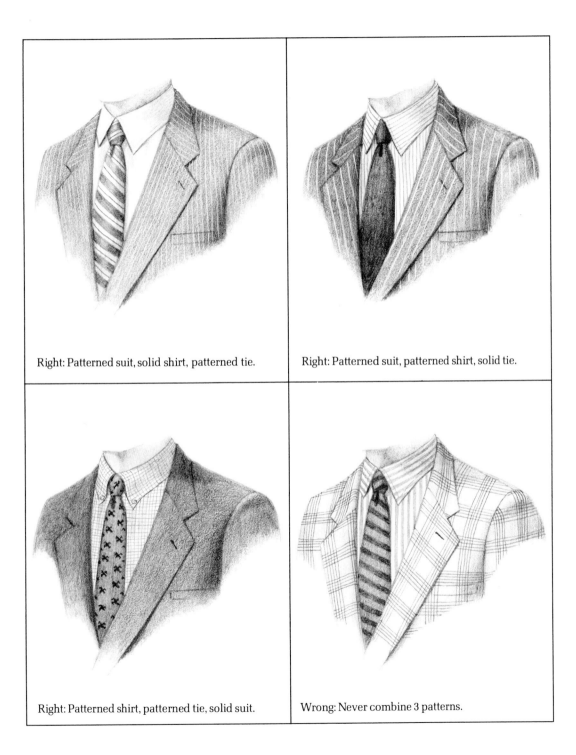

Right: Patterned suit, solid shirt, patterned tie.

Right: Patterned suit, patterned shirt, solid tie.

Right: Patterned shirt, patterned tie, solid suit.

Wrong: Never combine 3 patterns.

Here are examples of combining a patterned suit and shirt with a solid tie:

- Pinstriped suit; subtle hairline-striped or soft oxford-striped shirt; solid tie.
- Chalkstriped suit; subtle oxford-striped or thin-striped shirt; solid tie.
- Tweed sport coat; subtle tattersall checked shirt; solid tie.
- Herringbone suit; pale striped shirt; solid tie.

Here are examples of combining a solid suit, patterned shirt, and patterned tie:

- Solid suit; subtle hairline-striped shirt; striped or foulard tie.
- Solid suit; subtle oxford-striped shirt; irregularly wider-striped, foulard, or club tie.
- Solid suit; subtle plaid shirt; wider-striped or plaid tie, or ribbed knit where the texture appears patterned.
- Solid suit; subtle tattersall checked shirt; club tie.
- Solid suit; white-on-white shirt; any patterned tie.

Any patterned shirt that is *not* subtle should be worn with a solid tie.

DON'T: COMBINE THREE PATTERNS

There is no quicker way to ruin your image than to clutter yourself with too many patterns. You automatically draw the eye away from your face and call attention to the clothes. True, if you are terribly clever you might come up with some good pattern combinations. However, they will look better on the hanger than under your face. Each pattern competes with the other and the eye has to move around trying to decipher the picture. Your impact is diminished.

DO: STRIVE FOR CONTRAST

It always looks best to have contrast between suit and shirt, shirt and tie. Think how boring a man looks in a gray suit, a white shirt, and the same color gray tie. But change that tie to red, navy, black, or even charcoal gray, and you have an entirely different impression!

There are two ways to create contrast: dark and light, or light and bright. Some men need more contrast than others, depending on their season. A blue shirt with a medium blue tie offers medium contrast; a white shirt with a navy tie offers high contrast. The first is fine for Summers, the latter for Winters. All men need some degree of contrast to look exciting.

Contrast is the way to successfully pull off a monochromatic look. Mix a dark brown suit, beige shirt, and coffee tie—elegant. Even though the colors are all from the brown family, they offer varying degrees of intensity.

There are three basic combinations:

- With a dark suit, wear a light shirt and a bright, medium, or dark tie.
- With a medium suit, wear a light shirt and a dark tie.
- With a light suit, wear a medium shirt and a dark tie. A medium shirt might be an end-on-end weave, which is darker than an oxford cloth. Winters, who can't wear medium shirts, wear a white or striped shirt and a dark or brightish tie.

DO: COMBINE COMPATIBLE FABRICS

Fabric varies in three ways: weight, texture, and finish.

The *weight* of a fabric depends on its content and the density of its weave. In wool suits, winter weights can be heavy and thick (up to twelve ounces). The year-round wools are medium and thinner (eight to ten ounces). Lighter weights, called tropicals, are thin and may be wool, cotton, linen, or blends.

Texture is determined by the nubbiness of a fabric. Knits, tweeds, and corduroys are heavily textured. Worsteds, tightly woven wools, fine cotton, and silk are generally smooth in texture.

Finish has to do with the sheen of fabrics. Finishes range from such flat matte finishes as a flannel suit, an oxford cloth shirt, or a wool tie to the high sheen in a silk tie.

When combining the weight, texture, and finish of a coat or suit, shirt, and tie, keep *likes with likes.* Heavy goes with heavyish, nubby goes with matte, smooth goes with a sheen. A tweed jacket (nubby matte finish) goes with a knit (matte finish) wool tie, and a solid worsted suit (smooth) with a silk tie (sheen).

Here are examples of appropriate fabric combinations:

- A nubby tweed sport coat; an oxford cloth shirt; a medium-weight textured knit tie.
- A smooth worsted formal suit; a silk or fine broadcloth shirt; a silk tie.
- A lightweight poplin summer suit; either an oxford or broadcloth shirt; a cotton madras tie.
- Corduroy pants; a heavy flannel shirt.

In the springtime, when you bring out your lighter-weight, smooth-finish wool suit, it would be inappropriate to wear your heavy wool, loose-weave tie, even if the color is right. The weight and texture are wrong. That suit may be worn with either a tightly woven lightweight wool tie or a silk tie.

DON'T: MIX STYLES OF CLOTHING

Clothing automatically has a style. It is dressy or casual, woodsy or executive, city or country, faddish or classic, depending on its color, line, fabric, and pattern. Obviously you would not wear a corduroy jacket with your pinstriped pants. But there are subtler combinations that clash and ruin your image, too.

Color that is bright tends to be sporty, casual, or festive. Bright colors are only businesslike when used as accents, such as stripes in a tie. Pastels are fashion colors when worn in suits or sport coats, but are conservative in business shirts. Dark colors are classic business and traditional country sports colors.

Patterns can be either conservative or sporty. Subtle patterns are classic, bold ones are sporty. Plaid, paisley, and club tie patterns are sporty. Striped, polka-dot, and foulard patterns are more formal. However, some striped ties are casual, and some parsleys are more formal, depending on their colors, and their fabric.

Fabric is also dressy or casual. Knits and tweeds are sporty. Worsteds and silks are dressy. A silk shirt would never be worn with a nubby knit tie.

The *cut* or *styling line* of a garment determines a lot about its character. That is why a European cut suit in a fine flat wool and conservative color does *not* go with an oxford cloth button-down shirt. The styles clash, and so do the textures. The suit demands a clean line and a fine, smooth texture; the button-down has a chunky line and a rough texture. Similarly, bellbottom pants don't go with a tapered double-breasted blazer. A collar pin in a business shirt looks wrong with a tweed sport coat.

SUMMARY

Here is a summary of the do's and don'ts of successfully combining your coat, shirt, and tie:

- Do: Buy *only* colors from your chart
- Do: Combine three solids
- Do: Combine two solids with one pattern
- Do: Combine one solid with two noncompeting patterns
- Don't: Combine three patterns
- Do: Strive for contrast
- Do: Combine compatible fabrics
- Don't: Mix styles of clothing

Now that you know the rules for putting your clothes and your colors together, you are ready to begin refining your look and thinking about your personal style.

12

YOUR CLOTHING PERSONALITY

While attending a formal rehearsal dinner, I was introduced to some of the groom's college buddies who had flown in from New York for the occasion. All worked on Wall Street and all wore collar pins—popular in New York. One young man was a former football player, short and stocky, with sandy crew-cut hair and a rough, craggy face still sporting scars from his days on the field. His pink broadcloth, round-collared shirt with collar pin looked strikingly wrong. This ruggedly masculine face and body was out of character in such a formal, elegant, and fashion-oriented shirt. For him, a plain-collared broadcloth shirt—minus pin—would have looked formal, harmonious, and flattering.

What is your clothing personality? As you go through life you begin to get a feel for what clothing styles really are *you*. Perhaps you long for the David Niven country gentlemen look, but your body and face call for the John Wayne image—rugged and casual. Maybe you feel you must have a pinstriped suit, but you never feel good in it and never receive compliments while wearing it. There's a reason for this.

To really look good, your clothes must reflect not only your inner spirit but also your physical self. Doesn't it make sense that your coloring, your build, and your facial structure would play a part in determining your best clothing image? Inner spirit counts, too, but not to the point that you spoil your natural qualities by trying to be something you are not.

You don't ever have to wear anything that doesn't flatter you just to fit a mold. Whether it's a social or corporate image you seek, you can always dress appropriately without sacrificing your best look.

Your season gives you the first clue about your image because your coloring and the colors you wear automatically make a statement. In general, a Winter looks best in solid colors, sharp contrasts, and a crisp silhouette—a rather formal look. A Summer man is more flattered by gentler contrasts, subtler patterns, and slightly softer fabrics. The Autumn man, with his warm coloring, looks especially good in tweeds, plaids, and rich, nubby fabrics, sophisticated but casual, while Spring is best in informal, relaxed clothing, also textured but always youthful, with colorful striped or checked shirts and ties.

But what if you are a Winter with light brown hair, blue eyes, a slight build, and a boyish face? You might *not* look your best when dressed in formal three-piece suits with boldly striped ties. If you are a tall, slim Spring with elegantly refined facial features and smooth, white-blond hair, you are more formal and sleek than the casual Spring man described above.

So you need to take into consideration not only your seasonal coloring but also your size, body structure, and facial features.

CLOTHING TYPES

There are five basic clothing personality types: Dramatic, Romantic, Natural, Classic, and Gamin. These clothing images are not absolute and they may overlap, but depending on your individual personality, lifestyle, and work environment, you can use them to influence your clothing selections in order to look and feel your best.

Dramatic

You are a man of *design*, *style*, *detail*, and *sharp contrasts*. The dramatic man is authoritative, innovative, assertive. Everything about his appearance makes a bold statement; his clothes are of the latest fashion, but not faddish.

The man who can wear dramatic attire is usually tall and lean, sometimes very thin, with broad, horizontal shoulders. Your body tends to have long, vertical lines rather than a chunky look, and your hair is dark or strikingly blond or gray. Nothing about you is middle of the road. You have angular facial features, perhaps a sharply pointed nose or chin, and an angular body. You have a certain elegance about you, and walk with large strides and a confident air. You have built-in authority by virtue of your size and striking coloring. Your looks call for you to dress with authority, sophistication, and a degree of formality. In general, you wear bold or dark colors mixed with your season's white for maximum contrast. On you, more is still conservative. Relative to your size and coloring, more still looks like less. Even your hair can be a bit long, but must be styled and controlled, definitely in touch with the latest fashion.

BUSINESS CLOTHES: You can easily achieve the corporate image, but your tall, thin body just doesn't call for a two-piece sack suit. On you it looks dumpy. For business or dress you look best in a boldly structured silhouette, such as a European- or updated American-cut suit with a constructed shoulder (maybe even roped and squarish), an average width lapel, vertical seams in the jacket, a slightly fitted waist, and a vest. You may wear a single or double vent, depending on your personality and job environment. Your style calls for cuffless pants unless your legs are so long that you want to minimize them. For social occasions you may want to buy a double-breasted suit. If your work allows you the freedom to be a little more stylish, do so. On you, less conservative clothes still *look* conservative because they are in harmony with your body type.

You look best in a dark, solid three-piece suit in navy, charcoal gray, or brown, depending on your season, worn with crisp white or light shirts. You are also the perfect candidate for pinstriped suits—either one quarter or one half inch, whichever is more harmonious with your size. High-contrast prints—such as a light pinstripe on a dark background—are appropriately sharp on you, but you find most checks and plaids too blended or casual. A bold plaid in dark colors and a rough fabric could work for you. You don't wear tweeds well because they offer so little contrast, though a striking herringbone might be all right for variety.

You wear stiffer fabrics, such as heavy gabardine or smooth worsteds, with a firm finish and a crisp silhouette. No flannels for you—at least not the kind that look fuzzy. You're a formal fellow, really, and not very soft around the edges.

DRESSY SPORTSWEAR: You dress boldly in sportswear, too, and favor extremes—either solid, dark-colored blazers (maybe even double-breasted) or a heavily textured or patterned sport coat (say, a bold houndstooth check). Subtle tweeds just fade away on you. Pleated wool pants are great on you, though you can wear nonpleated slacks just as well. You will always wear wool or cotton pants rather than cords or jeans with your sport coat.

Dramatic

SHIRTS: You look best in a crisp, light shirt (solid white, light pastel, or icy) with a plain pointed collar, either regular or wide spread. Choose cotton broadcloth with a hard finish for the sharpest look. Also excellent on you are bold stripes, hairline stripes, and bold plaids. A colored shirt with a contrasting white collar and cuff might work—probably with a stripe, and usually best for Winters—and you may want to wear a collar pin once in a while. You practically never wear oxford cloth button-downs, knits, or checks or muted plaids. You tend to dress up a little more than the next fellow, and French cuffs are your thing.

TIES: Your ties must always make a strong statement and offer sharp contrast to your shirt, though you can also wear a monochromatic look with a shirt and tie from the same color family. Solid colors, especially dark or bright reds, are excellent. Your best patterns are stripes with bold contrasts, either a widely spaced pinstripe or widish stripes irregularly spaced. An overall geometric pattern is good. A foulard is usually not expressive enough for you, but it may work if you choose one with a repeat pattern of high contrast and sharp lines (diamonds rather than circles). Any dot pattern should be extreme, preferably with large dots—medium looks boring on you. Any pattern you choose should offer contrast within the tie. Plaids and checks are too casual for you, and club ties are too conservative. You look great in a silk tie with a sheen. One word of caution: be careful not to ruin your look with loud ties that are not tasteful. A dramatic look simply calls for more contrast, darker or brighter colors, straight rather than curved lines in patterns.

SHOES: For work, your shoes are smooth, highly polished oxfords with a medium to thin sole and a slightly pointed toe without wing tip. These shoes are okay for dressy sportswear, too, though you might want a dressy loafer.

CASUAL WEAR: The Dramatic man always likes to make a fashion statement and dresses in outfits. For horseback riding you have riding clothes; for on the court, tennis whites. Your casual clothes can be stripes or solids, again offering contrast, or brightly colored polo shirts. You are a man of extremes in texture and expression. If you are conservative, keep your casual clothes relatively formal with nonpleated slacks in wools (cold weather) or cottons and gabardines. Less conservative types can wear pleats and suspenders, baggy chinos, or funkier clothing. Jeans are your least best look just because they are so average. Wear designer jeans or tight jeans or baggy jeans. Choose sweaters of heavy cable knits or geometric patterns or stripes, either form-fitting or on the baggy side. If a pair of silk lounging pajamas and a smoking jacket really appeal to you, you know you have a Dramatic's flair.

COATS: Your topcoat might be either a dark double-breasted overcoat of cashmere or fine wool or a heavily textured wraparound with a tie belt. Your trenchcoat can't be ordinary. Skip the Burberry and go for something with a bold silhouette. Think oversize for coats. Wear anything big and bulky—you can carry it off! An extremely padded shoulder or a dropped shoulder make a strong fashion statement for you, and dark colors work well.

JEWELRY: Any jewelry you wear should look important. Your watch should be large rather than slimline, with either a textured leather or a metal band. You might wear a ring with a stone or large cuff links that make a statement. Nothing dinky for you.

FORMAL: A tuxedo looks great on you. If you are a Winter you'll stick to a black tux because it looks so dashing on you, but you could wear an unusual color— burgundy, dark navy, dark brown, or even a very light color, depending on your season.

DRAMATIC PROTOTYPES: Sean Connery, Errol Flynn, Clark Gable, Burt Lancaster, Ricardo Montalban, Charlton Heston, Jack Palance, George Hamilton

Romantic

You are the man who calls for a *rich, luxurious, well-blended* look. The Romantic is a Romeo—a lover, not a fighter. You're gracious and suave, with the air of an artist or poet about you. Very sensual and very social, you have expensive tastes and a bit of theatrical flair. Everything about you suggests wealth, sophistication, and the bedroom. The Romantic is a people person and can be found in highly visible positions—both at work and at play. In general, you're naturally interested in fashion and grooming, and you need to restrain your flamboyance rather than strive for an energetic look.

The Romantic man is moderately tall with an athletic but not overdeveloped build—strong but not bulky. Romantics tend to have beautiful eyes and skin and thick hair—curly, wavy, or straight, but always luxurious. Your face is expressive and well-proportioned, important to your overall look. Sophisticated and sexy, you're influenced by current fashions and have a love of soft fabrics and luxurious colors. A rather formal dresser, you choose clothes fitted to show off your body symmetry; all detail serves to frame your face.

BUSINESS CLOTHES: If you work in a field that allows for less conservative dress, you can really go for a high-fashion look. A fitted European-cut suit is your best look, with either double vents or no vent (a single vent is too boxy for you). Padded shoulders and a very suppressed waist flatter your lithe silhouette. A double-breasted jacket is good for you, too. If your profession requires a conservative image, choose the updated American-cut suit, with a suppressed waist and padded shoulder. Leave off the vest—it's a boring look for you. Avoid sharp lines in favor of a smooth, slightly curved silhouette. Choose fine wools and cashmere rather than stiff fabrics or gabardine. Soft, lightweight woolens suit your look and your expensive tastes. Your favorite textured fabric will be very soft; your favorite colors are the richest (not darkest) colors of your palette—lush colors of medium intensity such as rich navy or warm coffee brown. For suits, solids are best, though stripes in soft textures and woven-in designs can work well for you. Patterns, if any, should be in a small scale, and plaids aren't really for you.

DRESSY SPORTSWEAR: This is your best style—the clothes in which you are most comfortable. The Romantic favors elegant sportswear—a fitted cashmere jacket, for example. He avoids patterned sport coats or any highly contrasting separates. He wears trendy looks—Italian sportswear that is fitted to the body. Pleated pants are fine as long as they are fairly fitted in the hips and buttocks. You enjoy special jackets, such as one that's short and fitted in a buttery leather, or something long and draped and stylish. Soft wool, suede, and silk make excellent jackets for you.

SHIRTS: Since your face is one of your best features, unusual collars are your forte. Collar pins or lapel pins are excellent on you, as are round collars, wing collars, or any very high collars. For corporate attire, wear an unstarched standard collar in a thin, smooth broadcloth, and in other professions choose a fabric such

Romantic

as silk or cotton batiste. Avoid overly crisp shirts—they are cold for a Romantic. Do wear some color, rather than white, but stick mostly to solids. Stripes are not your best look unless they are very well-blended and soft. French cuffs suit your formal and sophisticated look.

TIES: Go for silk, either shiny or raw (matte), in a well-blended design—never a knit or woven tie. Solids are your absolute best. Since your overall look is harmonious, choose a tie that is in medium contrast to your shirt, either solids or a pattern that has colors from both your jacket and shirt. In patterns, stripes must be well-blended and paisleys are best in shiny silk with a watercolor effect. Foulards are not the Romantic's best look because they are too crisp and predictable. If you need them for corporate wear, choose repeat patterns in teardrop or oval shapes. Pin dots on shiny silk are good, but avoid medium or large dots. Avoid patterns with rigid structures or defined edges. Unusual ties—narrow ones, for example—are good.

SHOES: Never one to wear a heavy oxford or wing tips, you will choose a lightweight Italian-look shoe with a thin sole, or an elegant boot of very fine, soft leather or suede.

CASUAL WEAR: Both elegant and trendy, your casual wear should look expensive and reflect your sophisticated flamboyance. You wear designer jeans, smooth leather pants, wing-collared shirts, and fashion colors. Choose a short leather jacket with epaulets or a military jacket with lots of detail.

COATS: Overcoats must have shape and a fitted silhouette. Padded shoulders are important, and wrap belts work well. Choose soft woolens or cashmere if possible.

JEWELRY: Used as an accent and not overdone, jewelry is great on the Romantic man—a collar bar or a ring with a stone, for example, but no heavy neck chains. Your watch is a simple, but elegant, slim line with either a metal or smooth leather band. Think tasteful and subtle.

FORMAL: A truly formal look, though flattering, can look too severe on you. Although a fussy look doesn't suit you, you can take some liberties with your formal look—a jeweled lapel pin, a white tux, or a red tie and cummerbund. Tails and a fitted waist in your formal jacket work for you. If the occasion allows, try something different, such as a velvet jacket and silk shirt over designer jeans.

ROMANTIC PROTOTYPES: Christopher Atkins, Richard Gere, Michael Jackson, Sugar Ray Leonard, John Schneider, Omar Sharif, Billy Dee Williams, Michael York, Elvis Presley, Lorenzo Lamas

Natural
You are the man who calls for *textures, tweeds, informality,* and a *blended* look.

The Natural man is usually of sturdy or athletic build. Your face may be craggy with irregular features, or perhaps you have a square jaw and wide-set eyes or simply a rugged and outdoorsy look. You might have freckles, and your hair is rarely glossy. Your stride is easy and you have a down-to-earth look about you. The Natural is an informal dresser who is rarely comfortable all dressed up and gets the most compliments in jeans and sweaters. You look best in casual, relaxed clothing and in the colors from your palette that are closest to nature, especially the browns, greens, and blues. Your hair is loose and wavy, or short, straight, and layered—casual rather than overly controlled, and always with the dry look. And you're the guy who can wear a beard or mustache well.

BUSINESS CLOTHES: A two-piece suit is better for you than a three-piece, which looks overly formal and stuffy on you. Your suit should be fuller cut, with a relaxed shoulder. If you are athletic but thin, you will have to buy a slimmer cut suit, but it should not be tapered too much at the waist. You would never wear trendy cuts in suits.

Your best suits for work are solid flannels in a medium color, or perhaps a subtle glen plaid, check, tweed, or other pattern. Dark solids may look severe on you, and pinstripes are definitely too formal and stiff. (You *can* survive in the business world without owning a pinstripe!) At most you would wear a subtle chalk stripe, preferably in colors without much contrast.

Your best fabrics are heavyish with some texture and always a matte (nonshiny) finish or a nap: flannel, corduroy, and looser weaves. Nothing shiny, fancy, or too formal.

DRESSY SPORTSWEAR: If your work environment allows for slacks and sport coats, so much the better. You are better looking in a sport coat than in a suit.

Think texture. A corduroy jacket or a heavy wool, tweed, or check are your best looks. A camel jacket is ideal for you if you are an Autumn or Spring. Your best dress-up attire is sportswear whenever possible, and you can be quite natty in a country tweed with leather patches on the elbows and perhaps a turtleneck instead of a shirt and tie. Patch pockets and topstitching really are your look.

SHIRTS: You are best in oxford cloth for work and for social occasions except when the event calls for formal attire. Broadcloth is dress-up for you. Button-down collars are great for you, but no round collars or collar pins. They're too fancy and lack the masculinity needed to look harmonious with your face and body. Plaids and checks are your best patterns. Subtle, blended, broad stripes are okay, but no severe or formal hairline stripes.

TIES: You go for less sharp contrast in your coat, shirt, and tie combinations. The monochromatic look—using colors from the same color family in varying degrees of intensity—is ideal for the Natural. Your best tie patterns are plaids and checks or wide stripes in muted colors creating a blended look. Foulard ties with square designs are better than rounds or ovals. No dots for you—they're too formal. Paisleys are sophisticated yet natural, especially in the warm palettes, and are a good dress look for the Natural man. Texture and matte finishes are again wonderful. Ribbed knits, wools, nubby linen (in summer), and nonshiny silks are best.

SHOES: Shoes for the Natural are a dressy loafer for business and a more casual one for sportswear. You might wear a textured leather oxford with a heavy sole, wing tip, and topstitching, or perhaps even a saddle shoe with your tweed sport coat. Your shoes have a widish American toe rather than a European look.

CASUAL WEAR: Casual wear is your thing. You may prefer to wear the colors closest to nature in your palette, and you definitely wear natural fabrics such as linen looks and cotton. Wear khakis, cords, and jeans with turtlenecks, plaid flannel shirts, button-downs, or short-sleeved cottons and T-shirts for warm weather. As usual for you, plaids, checks, and solids in nubby fabrics are best. Your sweaters are crewnecks or bulky, textured pullovers. No argyles or fancy patterns. Nonshiny leather is best for boots, belts, or any accessories.

Natural

COATS: You may not want a topcoat because they're so formal, and you can wear your trenchcoat almost anywhere now anyway. If you do want a wool topcoat, choose a double- or single-breasted camel polo if you're a warm season, or a single-breasted beige or blue if you're a cool season. Shaggy furs or shearling suit you well, as do nonshiny leathers such as sheepskin. Your trenchcoat is either the single-breasted simple one with raglan sleeves or a traditional military trench with epaulets and heavy trim. If you are a thin and lanky Natural, forget the gewgaws; they'll overwhelm you.

JEWELRY: Jewelry, if any, would be heavy and masculine—but probably you don't wear any. Your watch should not be too thin, and could have a leather strap rather than a metal band.

FORMAL: A tuxedo is your least favorite item of clothing. Choose a simple pleated shirt in the color of your season and, if possible, a tuxedo in your color as well. For other social occasions, the Natural man can always dress in sportier attire than the Dramatic or Classic man. On you, a beautiful sport coat, wool slacks, a shirt, and a tie looks dressy. For weddings, funerals, and formal affairs, wear your suit in a medium color rather than a dark one.

NATURAL PROTOTYPES: Alan Alda, Harrison Ford, Bruce Jenner, Calvin Klein, Joe Namath, O. J. Simpson, John Wayne, Robert Redford, Tom Selleck, Clint Eastwood, Michael Landon, Robert Conrad, Gene Hackman, John Riggins

Classic

The Classic man's looks call for *simplicity, quality,* and *moderation.*

Your body is of average proportions, not too tall or short, neither lanky nor extremely muscular. Your facial features are evenly proportioned and regular, with no prominent features such as a big nose or a very square jaw. Your face has refined features and your coloring is medium. Everything about you is sophisticated and moderate. Your demeanor is conservative, poised, slightly formal, but not stuffy. Nothing you wear should be extreme in style, fabric, texture, or color. Simplicity of line and detail suit you best. You are the traditional type, a fashion conservative. Because you do not look good in fads, gimmicks, or high-fashion clothes, or in any form of bold or extreme patterns, you must rely on fine fabric and beautifully tailored, conservative clothes. You cannot get away with rumpled or ill-fitting clothing. You must look fastidious, even if it's not truly your nature. You look best with a relatively short, conservative hairstyle—always combed and neatly in place.

BUSINESS CLOTHES: For business you wear two-piece suits on most days, reserving three-piece suits for important meetings or dressy occasions. You wear the traditional Ivy League suit (Brooks Brothers) or, if you are slim, the updated American silhouette. Choose a suit with a relaxed, unstructured shoulder but slightly trimmer at the waist. You don't want topstitching or any sporty or faddish details.

Because Classic represents the middle value in body type, size, and coloring, you look great in most classic patterns as long as they are moderate in scale and contrast—a subdued pinstripe or chalk stripe, for example, or a small check or medium-scaled, subtle plaid. Your season dictates your best patterns: Winters in stripes, windowpanes, and herringbones; Summers in stripes and soft tweeds; Autumns in tweeds and plaids; Springs in plaids and checks. Solids are excellent for all.

Your best fabrics are light- to medium-weight worsteds or very thin, tightly woven flannels and tweeds with a firm finish.

DRESSY SPORTSWEAR: Your first sport coat is a solid single-breasted blazer in a nice wool fabric. Next is a herringbone or tweed in a fairly fine texture. You do not wear heavily textured or boldly patterned fabrics well, even in sportswear. Classic styles in wool slacks are for you—no exaggerated pleats, flared legs, or trendy items. You might wear tweed, checked, or plaid wool slacks for a bit of dash.

SHIRTS: You go for an understated look, and are best in white or solid pastel shirts (especially blue) in oxford button-down for day and broadcloth plain collars for evening or special occasions. For a natty look, you might wear a collar pin or a colored shirt with a white collar. You don't wear many patterned shirts, save an occasional subtle stripe or a white on white. Although plaids and checks are not your thing, you can wear a tattersall check with a solid blazer for sport. In general, you'll wear a shirt and tie rather than a turtleneck with your sport coat for special events.

Classic

TIES: Your tie is also conservative, but does not have to be dull. Foulard ties are your best pattern, with the repeats in oval or rounded shapes. You can wear thin, evenly spaced stripes, or irregular stripes in moderate widths and traditional colors. Club ties are great, especially with a sport coat, but most plaids or checks are too casual and sporty for you. A silk tie is your best fabric, though thin wools and linens (in summer) are fine, too. Either a matte or a slight sheen works well on you. A slight sheen is best as a dressy look. Never wear any loud or boldly patterned tie; there is nothing eccentric about your body, so you can't wear eccentric clothing.

SHOES: Shoes for business are lace-up oxfords with a medium sole and an American wide-cut toe, with or without wing tips. The leather can be smooth or lightly textured. If you're the elegant type, you might wear a smooth oxford with a European toe, especially for dress. For sportswear you wear your oxfords or a dressy loafer.

CASUAL WEAR: The Classic man's casual clothes are crisp and clean. Wool or cotton pants, ironed blue jeans (if any) with oxford cloth button-downs in the wintertime and polo shirts in the summertime. You might even be preppy and inclined toward plaid pants if you're not too conservative. Although you will probably not wear funky, way-out colors in sport shirts, you can wear fun colors in basic reds, blues, greens, and yellows.

COATS: Your best topcoat is a single-breasted wool with simple details—no topstitching, epaulets, etc. Your trenchcoat may be single- or double-breasted, but again with simple styling and no gimmicks. The traditional Burberry coat is your look as well.

JEWELRY: Jewelry for the Classic is tasteful, refined, and minimal. A thin watch with a metal or smooth leather band works well for you. A class ring is okay, but no bracelets or neck chains.

FORMAL: You look great in a tuxedo because it gives you the opportunity to dress like a Dramatic but within the confines of tradition. You look better in average lapels rather than the ones that point upwards toward the shoulder.

Choose pleated shirts rather than ruffles. You also look great dressed up in a three-piece suit, which adds variety to your usual two-piece or business look.

CLASSIC PROTOTYPES: Richard Crenna, John Forsythe, Cary Grant, Gregory Peck, Phil Donahue, Robert Young, Henry Fonda, Bing Crosby, Anthony Perkins, Jerry Brown, John Glenn, Bryant Gumbel

Gamin

You are the man whose look is *dapper, natty, crisp* and very *structured*. The Gamin man, small in stature, is flashy and full of energy, and is by nature quite precise about the way he dresses.

The Gamin has a boyish face and body and a jaunty stride, and is perpetually young-looking. You are a rather formal dresser and tend to be trendy and fashion conscious with an eye for detail. You need to buy smaller patterns, scaled to your size so they don't overwhelm your look. Though youthful-looking, your clothes are always fitted and neat. Your hair may be curly and tousled or straight and layered, but a long, slick style is not for you.

BUSINESS CLOTHES: You look great in a three-piece updated American cut suit, especially in a bright and crisp glen plaid. Small patterns such as herringbones are great. The Gamin man can wear solids for contrast to his patterned shirts and ties. He should avoid dull, dark colors. Pinstripes are too rigid for you, but an irregular stripe might work. Choose stiff, crisp fabrics—tightly woven worsteds, gabardines, or cotton blends.

DRESSY SPORTSWEAR: A jacket and dress slacks is a great look for the effervescent Gamin, since he favors a look that's youthful, fitted, and fashionable. Strive for a crisp, snappy look—say, your season's navy blazer, white pants, and an argyle sweater vest. Choose hard-finish wool fabrics, crisp cottons, or corduroys and keep your tweeds, checks, and plaids in small scale. You look great in touches of color, such as stripes or checks in sportswear and casual clothes. Combining patterns, such as a striped shirt and striped tie, is a smart look for you.

SHIRTS: Gamins choose colors more than whites, and also favor plaids and checks with contrast rather than a muted look. Colorful stripes work well on you, as do tattersalls, and colored or patterned shirts with a contrasting white collar.

Gamin

You would choose a pattern over a solid most of the time, except with a patterned suit. Always wear crisp, neatly pressed cottons and strive for high contrast in your clothing combinations.

TIES: In patterns, choose colorful stripes or club ties with a highly contrasting motif. Use solid-color ties to offer high contrast and a snappy accent to a patterned shirt or suit. Choose a matte rather than a shiny finish. Avoid pin dots—they're too formal, but a medium dot might work for you. Foulards work if the pattern offers colorful contrast. Squares are better than ovals. A Gamin is the man who can successfully wear a bow tie.

SHOES: You'll probably want a dressy loafer for business and perhaps a more casual pair for sportswear. Gamins love detail. Wear tassels and buckles on your shoes.

CASUAL WEAR: Gamins will go for color in their casual wear, used as stylish accent or detail. You are a pressed and organized dresser even in your casual wear. Wear argyle sweaters, pleated pants, and saddle shoes. Cuffed pants look good on you because they add crisp lines. (Don't worry if your legs are short—your total look is more important.) You need a broken, staccato look because of your compact size and high energy level. In casual wear, you can break the rules and get out of scale with wide stripes and wide-wale cords.

COATS: Choose a style that's trim and sharp-looking, such as a double-breasted trenchcoat or a wool topcoat in solid or small tweed with set-in rather than raglan sleeves. Epaulets are especially good for the Gamin.

JEWELRY: Gamins may wear a neck chain or ID bracelet, but always something restrained. You're too precise to enjoy a large or fancy ring, for example.

FORMAL: You can wear a dark tuxedo well (especially if you're a Winter), since on you the contrast with the shirt looks lively. Although you are an impeccably correct dresser, you hate to be conventional. For variety, try a tux in your color, wear a vest instead of a cummerbund, or try a plaid cummerbund and tie.

GAMIN PROTOTYPES: Johnny Carson, Sammy Davis, Jr., Dudley Moore, Richard Pryor, Joel Grey, Richard Simmons, Dick Cavett, Dick Clark, Red Buttons, Roddy McDowall, Fred Astaire

YOUR OWN BEST LOOK

Many men can look believable in more than one look. Paul Newman's image in a fisherman knit sweater is just as credible as his lawyer image in a three-piece suit. Warren Beatty can smooth his hair into a conservative, traditional style and go to work at IBM, or wear his hair wavy and loose and hang out in cords and sweaters, *or* dress in structured European suits and look dramatic. His looks are so versatile that simply by changing his hair and his demeanor he can pull off almost any clothing image.

Whatever image you favor, just be sure it's believable on you. You have undoubtedly seen someone whose clothing was socially acceptable but looked all wrong on *him*. Give yourself permission not to buy a tweed sport coat for variety if you're a formal Winter who will always look best in a solid blazer. Skip the pinstripe if you're a rugged outdoorsman caught in the trappings of a corporate work environment. No one will ever notice that you don't own a pinstripe. They'll just know that you always look nice in what you *do* have.

Understanding your clothing personality takes time and some experimenting. But now that you are aware of these general types, you can think a bit more about what really looks good on you the next time you buy clothes.

DRAMATIC TYPE

BUSINESS

Suits
Square shoulders
Suppressed waist
Single, double, or no vent
Two- or three-piece
Peaked or notched lapels
Worsted wools
Gabardine
Silk blends
Solids
Bold herringbone
Large box check
Windowpane
Bold plaid (design, not color)
Pinstripe—¼ or ½ inch

Shirts
Broadcloth
Solids
Thin stripe (crisp)
Wide stripe
Plain or spread collar
French cuffs

Ties
Silk—sheen
Dark solids
Large-scale patterns
Stripes—sharp contrast
Overall geometrics
Foulard (high contrast)

Accessories
Collar pin
Cuff links
Large watch
Suspenders

CASUAL

Sport Coats
Square shoulders
Single- or double-breasted
May be unconstructed
Smooth or very nubby
Wool, cotton, silk, blends
Solids
Heavy tweeds
Houndstooth

Pants
Wool, cotton, firm weave
Plain or pleated
Plain or cuffed
Straight or tapered

Shirts
Broadcloth
Solids
Bold plaid
Bold stripes

Sportswear
Costumes (outfits that fit activity)
Suspenders
Bulky knit sweaters
Lounging attire
Polo shirts—bright
Stripes, geometric patterns

ROMANTIC TYPE

BUSINESS

Suits
   Padded shoulders
   Suppressed waist
   Double or no vent
   Single- or double-breasted
   Two-piece
   Soft wools, silks, blends
   Solids
   Subtle stripes
   Woven-in designs

Shirts
   Broadcloth, silk, batiste
   Solids
   Stripe—subtle, blended
   Plain or rounded collars

Ties
   Silk—sheen
   Medium-color solids
   Medium-scale patterns
   Stripes—wide, blended
   Foulard—rounded patterns
   Paisley

Accessories
   Collar pin
   Stickpin
   Rings
   Thin chains
   Slimline watch

CASUAL

Sport Coats
   Square or natural shoulders
   May be unconstructed
   Single- or double-breasted
   Smooth textures
   Wool, silk, blends, leather
   Solids

Pants
   No-wale corduroy, leather
   Pleated or plain
   No cuffs
   Tapered

Shirts
   Silk, batiste
   Solids
   Unusual collars

Sportswear
   Italian styling
   Short, fitted jackets
   Velour warm-ups
   Soft sweaters

NATURAL TYPE

BUSINESS

Suits
Natural shoulders
Full-cut
Slightly suppressed waist (if thin)
Single vent
Single-breasted
Two-piece
Flannel, cotton, linen
Tweed
Herringbone
Large box check
Glen plaid
Subtle chalk stripe
Plaid

Shirts
Oxford cloth
Stripes—wide, subtle
Checks
Tattersall
Button-down

Ties
Silk—matte
Ribbed knit
Heavy wool
Linen
Medium-color solids
Medium-scale patterns
Stripes—wide, blended
Foulard—square designs
Club
Paisley
Plaid

Accessories
Watch with leather band

CASUAL

Sport coats
Natural shoulders
Single breasted
Nubby textures
Wool, cotton, linen, blends, corduroy, seersucker
Heavy tweed
Houndstooth
Plaid
Elbow patches
Patch pockets
Topstitching

Pants
Wool, cotton, corduroy, denim
Plain or pleated
Plain or cuffed
Straight or tapered

Shirts
Oxford, blends, flannel
Stripes—wide
Plaid
Checks

Sportswear
Turtlenecks
Vests
Bulky sweaters
Boots
Athletic outfits

CLASSIC TYPE

BUSINESS

Suits
Slightly padded shoulders
Slightly suppressed waist or full cut
Single or double vent
Single-breasted
Two- or three-piece
Worsted, flannel, cotton, blends
Solids
Tweed
Herringbone
Small box check
Windowpane
Glen plaid
Pinstripe—⅛ to ¼ inch
Chalk stripe

Shirts
Oxford or broadcloth
Solids
Subtle stripes
Tattersall
Button-down or plain collar

Ties
Silk—sheen, matte
Wool—smooth
Linen
Medium to dark solids
Medium-scale patterns
Stripes—thin, even or medium, un-
    even
Foulard—rounded, geometric
Club

Accessories
Watch—metal or leather band
Class ring
Collar pin

CASUAL

Sport Coats
Slightly padded to natural shoulder
Single- or double-breasted
Smooth textures
Solids
Subtle tweed, plaid
Houndstooth

Pants
Wool, cotton, corduroy (stiff)
Plain or cuffed
Straight legs

Shirts
Oxford, blends
Solids
Tattersall
Button-down

Sportswear
Polo shirts
Plaid pants
Nautical motifs

GAMIN TYPE

BUSINESS

Suits
Slightly padded shoulders
Slightly suppressed waist
Single vent
Single-breasted
Two- or three-piece
Worsted, cotton, blends
Gabardine
Solids
Tweed
Herringbone
Small box checks
Glen plaid
Pinstripe—⅛ inch

Shirts
Broadcloth
Solids
Thin crisp stripes
Checks
Tattersall
Plain or button-down collar

Ties
Silk—matte
Ribbed knit
Wool—smooth
Linen
Bow ties
Medium-color solids
Small-scale patterns
Stripes—sharp and/or colorful
Foulard—square, crisp
Club
Plaid

Accessories
Watch—leather band
ID bracelet

CASUAL

Sport Coats
Slightly padded shoulder
Single-breasted
Wool, cotton, linen, corduroy
Smooth to slightly nubby
Solids
Subtle tweed
Seersucker
Small plaid
Topstitching
Patch pockets

Pants
Cotton, wool gabardine, corduroy, denim
Pleated or plain
Straight leg

Shirts
Broadcloth, oxford, blends
Solids
Checks
Tattersall
Plaid

Sportswear
Sweater vest
Argyle patterns
Saddle oxfords

SHOPPING

Most men dislike shopping for two reasons. They resent the time involved and they feel unsure of their choices. The Color for Men System will cut your shopping time to a minimum. And you won't waste any money on a mistake. If you've been depending on someone else to select your clothes, or have simply been buying the same items year in and year out, now's the time for you to discover how to enjoy speedy, successful shopping.

Here are some tips to help make shopping efficient and rewarding.

Shop with your colors and look only at items in your colors.
Always shop with your color chart or fabric swatches. Your eye cannot retain the memory of a color for more than a few seconds. You may think you've spotted your red tie, only to find when you get home that it's the wrong red. Hold your chart or swatch against the garment in question. If it blends, it's yours. If it clashes, put it back.

Your palette works as a general guide, but be particularly careful when choosing colors that are difficult for you to wear. Winters should match their taupe (gray-beige) and lemon yellow closely. Summers should match their light lemon yellow and rose-beige as closely as possible, too. Autumns must take care with their marine navy and periwinkle, and Springs should match their grays and navies closely. Here fabric swatches will be your best guide, as it is difficult to reproduce colors in print with extreme accuracy.

Store lights often distort colors, so look at the item under natural light if possible.

When buying a patterned garment—plaid or tweed, for example—make sure the fabric falls within your palette by comparing its overall background color to your solid-color swatch. The effect should be the same in both.

It's okay if some of the pattern includes bits of colors that are not yours (see Neil, p. 27). The rule of thumb is not to let that off color ruin your total look. Bear in mind the following:

1. Don't allow the wrong color to dominate.
2. Don't allow the wrong color to force you to buy a tie, belt, or shoes in the wrong color.
3. Don't wear the wrong color near your face.

For example, a thread that is not your color may be woven through the background of a suit. That's okay as long as you don't buy a tie of that color. (It will often limit your tie selection.) Or you may find a pair of plaid slacks that contains colors from more than one season. Fine, as long as you can pull *your* color out for your shirt.

Say no to clothes that aren't in your colors.

Learn to say "no" to items that are not in your colors. Discipline yourself not to even look at them. Decisions will then be easy, you'll save time, and you guarantee yourself a coordinated wardrobe with myriad clothing combinations. The minute you add one off-color item, you complicate your wardrobe plan, and getting dressed will be that much harder.

Recognize when a bargain is not a bargain.

By saying "yes" only to sale items in your colors, you can be assured that everything you buy will go with whatever you own now or buy next year. Anything you buy on sale that doesn't look good on you is really a waste of money, not a saving.

Be aware of the clothing industry's color cycles and be open-minded about which color you want to buy.

Don't shop with a preconceived idea of a color you want to buy. Instead, be open-minded about what's available in your colors. The clothing industry does not promote every color every year. With the exception of basic business colors—navy, gray, tan—most colors come in cycles several years apart. If you are hankering to try out your emerald green polo shirt but you don't see that particular shade of green in the stores, forget it for now. You'll just be wasting your time hunting for it. Choose something in vogue now, as long as it's your color. Next year emerald green will probably be everywhere!

Your season will usually be your best shopping time of year. In springtime the light tan suits appear, the suits best for the Spring man. Dark blue-red blazers appear at Christmastime—good for the Winter man. During your off-season you may have to search for some of your colors. Stock up during your best shopping season on shirts and even suits in your colors that you can wear year-round.

Find a salesperson who is your season.

Any salesperson, male or female, automatically likes his or her own colors. Unless you are in a store where the personnel have been specifically trained to understand color, the salesperson is likely to sell you his or her colors instead of yours. Even with your chart or swatches handy, he or she is likely to "see" his or her blue instead of your blue. A salesperson who is your season will intuitively be of more help to you.

By the same token, shopping with a wife or friend who is not your season can produce the same unhappy results. Don't shop with a friend or spouse unless you're sure he/she understands *your* colors.

Find your store.

The buyer in a store influences the selection of all the merchandise. If the buyer is your season, you're in luck. She/he will intuitively select not only lots of your colors but also styles, fabrics, and patterns that suit you, too.

Furthermore, get to know which labels are cut and styled for you. Some stores will carry your cut; others won't.

Dress appropriately; be well groomed.

If you are shopping for jeans, it's fine to wear jeans and sneakers to the store. If you want to buy a suit, *wear* a suit! Not only do you need the shirt and shoes for a proper fit but it's also impossible to judge the look of even the finest suit when you're wearing a pair of old sneakers. Wear a solid tie, and chances are it will go with the suit. You can assess an outfit more successfully if you look the part. Comb your hair and shave. You will command the attention of the store personnel and therefore receive better service. A scruffy customer hardly looks like a good bet to a top-notch salesman.

Spend the most money on the clothes you wear the most.
If you wear a suit once a year, buy an inexpensive suit. But a suit worn every day won't hold its shape or wear well unless the fabric and tailoring are both of good quality. In this case, it's a waste of money to buy an inexpensive suit.

Develop a shopping routine.
First go to your size. If you're not sure of your size, have the salesperson measure you. Then pull out everything in your colors. Next choose the style and pattern. Check fabric and quality. Now try on. Last, call the tailor. For extra attention to your needs, tip the tailor from $5 to $10 each time you buy a suit. This habit assures you of special attention to your $300 to $500 purchase.

This shopping routine helps you to quickly sort out the possibilities. If nothing passes the first few steps, go to another store. You've put in little effort, and you still have the time, energy, and money to go elsewhere.

Once you buy a suit, have the tailor give you a swatch of the material after the suit is fitted. Keep your swatches on a large safety pin and hang the pin on your tie rack. When you shop, you can take the swatches along to remind you of the suits you already have, as well as to help you pick out new shirts and ties.

Make a list.
Using the Survival List in Chapter 6, itemize the clothing that you need to complete your wardrobe. If money is an issue, arrange the list in order of priority. Perhaps you need a topcoat and a suit, but both are expensive. Decide which you need more and put it at the top of the list. Shopping with a list prevents hit-or-miss impulse purchases that eat up your budget and keep you from being able to buy that second item that you really need.

It's also a good idea to tack a piece of paper and a pen to your closet door. When you notice you need some item of clothing, jot it down. When it's time to shop, your list is already compiled.

Clean your closet.
Go through your closet and remove everything you haven't worn for a year. If you haven't worn it for a whole year, chances are you never will. Give those clothes away. Automatically you will be removing clothes that don't fit, that are out of style, or that you simply don't like.

If your weight fluctuates, remove the wrong-size-for-now clothes and put them in a box or storage closet for a later date. Keep in your closet only the clothes you really wear. An organized closet simplifies getting dressed and leads to an organized day.

To avoid all that wasted space at the bottom of your closet, have a carpenter install a second closet pole halfway between the floor and the standard pole. Hang your shirts and coats on the top pole, your pants on the bottom. Put your robe on a hook. You also might want to build in cubbies for your shoes or folded shirts and sweaters.

Shop twice a year.

The clothing industry promotes warm-weather clothes beginning in January and cool-weather clothes in July, both following midwinter and midsummer sales. If you wait to buy summer clothes in the summertime, forget it. There's nothing left. In March or April buy everything you need for the spring and summertime. In August buy all your fall and winter clothes. During these months the selection is good, and you can purchase everything on your list in four hours or less, including trips to different stores for shoes or whatever. Add a couple of hours for return trips for fittings and you've got shopping down to ten hours or less per year.

By buying ahead of need you will never have to give up your Saturday golf or tennis because you were invited to a party Saturday night.

WHEN SOMEONE SHOPS FOR YOU . . .

If you really hate to shop, you can give your favorite woman or salesperson the Survival List and your color chart. If you are color-blind, you will have to let someone help you find your colors.

Many stores and image consultants, including our Color for Men consultants, offer personal shopping as a professional service. These professionals do the legwork for you, so all you have to do is try things on.

Shopping may never be your favorite pastime, but your colors certainly make it easier and less time-consuming. I know some men who've become shopping converts now that the frustration has been removed. Also, many men have had the selection of their clothes controlled by other people since their early childhood years. You might now enjoy having the freedom to shop for yourself, buying clothes that you like and knowing that you will look better than ever!

At the back of this book I have included shopping summaries grouped by season. Tear out your season's guide and keep it as a handy reference.

14

THE FINISHING TOUCHES: HAIR, GLASSES, AND GROOMING

HAIRSTYLE AND FACE SHAPE

No program to improve your looks is complete without attention to your hair. We've all seen the man who is well dressed and yet still doesn't look pulled together. A shaggy haircut (or an unkempt beard) can ruin the effect. Not only does a flattering haircut strengthen your best facial features and hide your flaws, but it also enhances your overall image. And a poor haircut does the opposite.

Finding the best hairstyle is harder for a man than for a woman. While women have flexibility, men can make only subtle adjustments in their hairstyle. In most businesses, hair must be relatively short; even so, the variation of a quarter inch in length can transform your face. The placement of your part, the length of the hair around your ears, a layered or blunt cut—all make a significant difference in your look.

Your best hairstyle depends on your face shape, the type of hair (curly, straight, thin, thick), your lifestyle, and the amount of time and care you're willing to devote to your hair. To decide how to get the cut that is best for you, let's see what face shape you have and how to work with it. There are seven basic shapes: oval, diamond, round, square, rectangle, oblong, and triangle. Pull your hair back from your face, look in the mirror, and examine the outline. Then choose from the following the category that most closely fits your face. You probably won't fit into an exact category, but having a sense of your general face shape will help you decide on a good haircut.

Oval

This is the "perfect" face shape. Slightly wider at the forehead than at the cheekbones or chin, it is classically proportioned.

If you have an oval face you can wear any hairstyle that suits your personality and lifestyle. Don't be afraid to change and experiment with new looks, for you can carry them off.

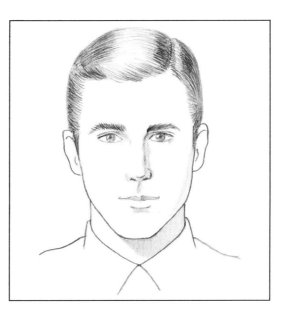

Diamond

A diamond face is wider at the cheek-bones than at the forehead or chin.

If your face is diamond-shaped, your hair should fill out your face at the forehead and chin while being close to your head (but not plastered flat) at its widest point.

When your hair covers your fore-head, your face seems wider. Fullness just below the back of the ears and in the back of the head gives weight to the chin and lower jaw area. Never pull your hair straight back. Use a slightly high side part. If your hair is curly, make sure it does not stick out at the temples.

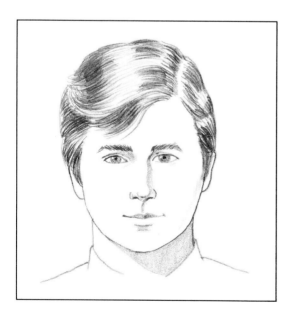

Round

A round face is also wider at the cheekbones but has a curved, chin and brow. It is almost as wide as it is long.

Your goal is to slim your face and create a longer look. Your hair can also help create the illusion of angles. Part your hair about two inches to either side of center with bangs on an angle to cut the roundness of your fore-head. Keep fullness at the top and around eye level, but trim hair shorter at the ears. Wear your sideburns a touch longer and cut them on an angle with the front pointing downward. A closely trimmed beard shaped on an angle can effectively slim a round face.

Square

A square face is about as wide at the cheeks as it is long, with an angular jaw and a square forehead.

If your face is square, your goal is to make your face seem a little longer and somewhat less angular. Keep your part 1½ inches to either side of center, as a part too far to the side accents squareness. Hair should be full on top, adding height. Cover the corners of your angular forehead with bangs that wave outward at both temples. Enjoy your square jaw. It's a masculine trait that many men envy.

Rectangle

Longer than it is wide, the rectangular face is square-jawed and has an angular forehead.

If your face is rectangular, you can shorten it slightly by adding fullness to the sides and softening the hairline. Cover your forehead with some off-center bangs to shorten your face and camouflage your angular forehead. A layered cut adds width and helps create roundness at the sides of your face. Blow-dry your hair to add fullness. Avoid long hair in the back.

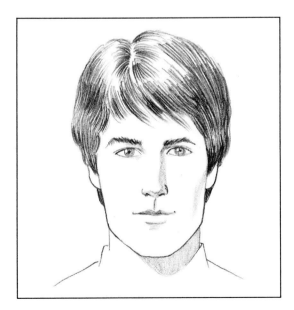

Oblong

The oblong face has the same proportions as the rectangular face, but the chin and brow are curved and rounded, not angular.

If you have an oblong face, you want to create the illusion of a shorter, fuller shape. Add fullness at the temples and sides, and keep it longer around the ears. A longish layered cut provides fullness especially if you blow-dry your hair. Keep it short at the back so the hairline doesn't drag the eye downwards.

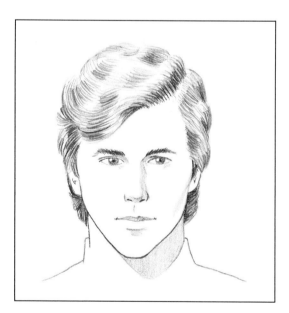

Triangle

A wide brow, slightly narrower cheekbones, and a narrow chin are characteristic of the triangular face.

If your face is triangular, you need to narrow your brow area and widen your chin. Part your hair about three inches to either side of center with bangs covering one side of the forehead. Keep it close-cropped at the top and temples, with extra length and fullness in the back, perhaps showing beneath the ears. A beard can be the perfect solution for filling in a narrow chin.

GOING, GOING, GONE: BALD CAN BE BEAUTIFUL, TOO

If you have thinning hair or are bald, don't despair. Yul Brynner and Telly Savalas have made baldness a symbol of virility, and Burt Reynolds and others have shown us that a hairpiece or transplant can be convincingly real. There are many options, and it is as important for you to know how to cut and take care of your hair as it is for the bushy-haired college kid.

Keeping your hair *short* is the trick. Identify your facial shape and emphasize its assets. A good cut and the use of a blow dryer to create fullness are essential. Remember:

- Keep thinning hair fairly short and always neatly trimmed. Long strands look sparse and *accentuate* baldness. Short, layered hair looks fuller than long hair.
- Never part your hair over one ear and comb long strands over your bald spot. It only calls attention to your baldness and looks terrible when the wind blows. Really, bald *is* attractive if you will work with it instead of trying to cover it up.
- If you have only a receding hairline, you *can* comb your hair forward. This does not look artificial, since some people wear their hair back to front anyway.
- If you have just a few hairs on the top of your otherwise bald head, shave them off. It looks neater, smoother, and sexier, and calls less attention to the top of your head.
- Consider growing a mustache or a beard if your professional life permits. Facial hair can often balance baldness.

HOW TO BLOW-DRY YOUR HAIR

If your hair is thinning or straight you can increase its fullness with a blow-drier. First lift hair with a round brush and blow hot air *against* the direction of hair growth. After you have held the dryer near the roots for a few seconds, wrap your hair around the brush in the direction you want it to fall and blow it almost dry on the brush.

If your hair is full, you need control, not more fullness. Use a warm (not hot) setting, and blow-dry in the same direction the hair grows. Simply blow as you brush. You need a regular, not a round, brush.

To control curliness, blow hair partially dry all over. Once hair is almost dry, use a brush to pull your hair flat and straight as you continue drying.

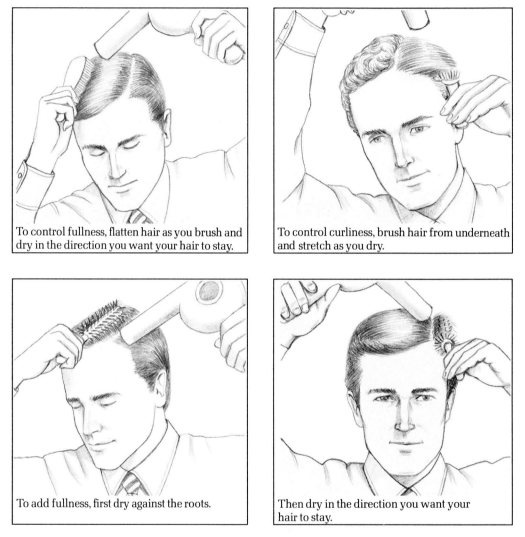

To control fullness, flatten hair as you brush and dry in the direction you want your hair to stay.

To control curliness, brush hair from underneath and stretch as you dry.

To add fullness, first dry against the roots.

Then dry in the direction you want your hair to stay.

To tame cowlicks, wrap hair around a brush in the desired direction. Hold firm and dry. Don't cut your cowlick too short or you won't be able to control it. Don't blow against the direction of the hair at the root, since it already sticks up.

For freestyle, rotate the dryer around your head, first blowing air against hair, then blowing with your hair's natural fall. Shake your head every couple of minutes to give your hair bounce.

HAIR COLOR

Some men do color their hair. The most common reason for coloring is to cover gray. The secret to success is having the results look natural. Depending on your season and situation, you may want to stay gray or cover your gray partly or completely.

Winters and *Summers*, the cool seasons, may prefer to stay gray, since gray often arrives attractively on the Winter or Summer man. Winters often gray early and beautifully. Unless you feel negative about gray hair, leave it alone. It's bright and beautiful.

Autumns and *Springs*, on the other hand, may prefer to cover their gray until it has completely arrived. During the two-tone stage, their gray tones may diminish their overall warm look. Once the gray is completely in, however, it has a yellowish cast and looks harmonious.

When selecting hair products or having your hair professionally colored, stick as closely as possible to your own hair color. Because of the peroxide they contain, many products bring out the red in your hair. Autumns and Springs don't need to worry about this, since red or golden tones look great on them, but Winters and Summers should avoid warm tones.

Color Guidelines

Here are guidelines for selecting the right color:

- Winters and Summers need tones with a cool base. Browns are good if they do *not* have the word "warm" in the name. Ash tones are for you.
- Autumns and Springs need tones with a warm base. Autumns can use warm brown, red, and auburn tones. Springs use golden brown, golden blond, or warm brown.

Application Tricks

Julius, Nancy Reagan's hairdresser, offers these tips for covering gray:

- Choose a light, natural shade that matches the lighter strands of your hair.
- When using comb-through products, don't apply the color all over. Dip the comb in the color, then comb it through for a natural look.

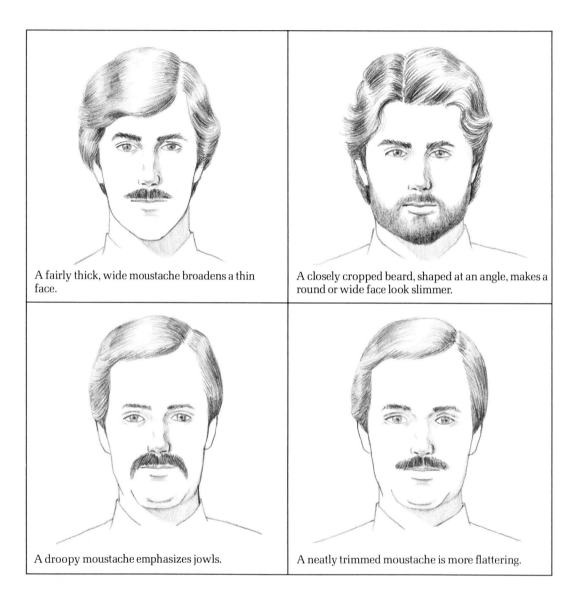

A fairly thick, wide moustache broadens a thin face.

A closely cropped beard, shaped at an angle, makes a round or wide face look slimmer.

A droopy moustache emphasizes jowls.

A neatly trimmed moustache is more flattering.

FACIAL HAIR

Beards or mustaches can create the illusion of a better face shape. Thin faces fill out, round or broad faces appear more chiseled. The line of the beard or mustache creates the illusion, so it's important to know what will work for you. Make sure any facial hair is well-trimmed and not exaggerated. Remember, facial hair influences your image. A shaggy, less stylized look is Natural. A Dramatic personality will want a more stylized look. A Classic type rarely wears facial hair, but if he does it must be neat and trim. Facial hair, especially beards, is usually not an acceptable corporate look.

If your beard color is distinctly different from your hair color, you may want to skip the beard. It gives you "two" seasons, and it's hard to look harmonious with your clothes when there are two different colors on your face.

GLASSES

The three factors to consider when selecting glasses are color, shape, and size. Select your glasses *after* you have your hair styled, as you want the frames to complement the new shape of your face. Also, if you plan to color your hair for any reason, do it before you buy glasses. The choice of frame color is affected by your hair color.

Choosing the Right Color Frames

The correct color of frames for you is based on your season and hair color. When buying plastic frames, choose the same color as your hair, but one shade lighter. If you are pale or sallow-skinned, do choose plastic frames, which bring color to your face. Autumns in particular should consider this option.

Winters and *Summers*, the cool seasons, should make sure that their frames—particularly brown ones—are not reddish or golden. Even tortoise-shell must be a cool brown. If you choose metal frames, they should be silver-toned.

Autumns and *Springs*, the warm seasons, should choose plastic frames with a warm red or golden tone. Metal frames should be gold-toned.

Color Tints for Lenses

The best color choices for tinted sunglasses, eye doctors say, are dark gray, green, and brown. Choose the correct tint for your season—gray for the cool seasons, brown or green for the warm seasons. Avoid colors such as blue (which makes it difficult to distinguish the color of traffic signals); lavender, orange, and rose (which don't screen out enough light to protect your eyes); and yellow (which actually intensifies the light).

For regular tinted glasses, choose no more than a 10 percent tint. It is fashionable now, and attractive, to tint the top of the lenses in a neutral 30 percent tint (say gray or brown, depending on your season), leave the center plain, and tint the bottom in a 10 to 20 percent tint. The effect is very subtle and very flattering, but leaves your eyes free to see naturally out of the center of your glasses.

Choosing the Right Shape

Glasses should complement the shape of your face. Choose frames that follow the shape of the top of your brow. The heaviness of the frames should be scaled to your bone structure.

You can adjust the width of the glasses frame for best effect. For most faces, keep the frames the same width as your temple. Choose them a *little* narrower to compensate for a wide face, or a *little* wider for a narrow face. Too narrow and they'll look dinky. Too wide and you'll look cartoonish!

Earlier in this chapter you identified your basic face shape. Here are some tips for selecting frames to suit your face shape.

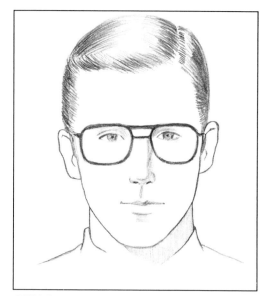

OVAL

DIAMOND

An oval face can wear any frame that is not extreme. Anything too large, too small, or too angular will look unbalanced. Choose a style that suits your bone structure, clothing personality, and season.

The diamond face wants to create the illusion of a wider chin line and forehead. You need frames with width on top, straightish sides, and bottoms that point downward and outward. Aviator glasses are excellent.

ROUND

A round face needs to create the illusion of cheekbones with frames that are straight across the top, angle inward toward the bottom, and square off across the bottom. Avoid round glasses or curved sides, which will emphasize roundness. Severely square glasses are also wrong because the contrast in shapes is too extreme.

SQUARE

Slightly rounded or curved frames with height on top can modify a too-square face. Since you want to lengthen the look of your face, aviator frames are handsome if your cheekbones are pronounced and gravity has not yet begun to make you jowly.

RECTANGLE

A rectangular face, being long and square, needs added width. A wide, square frame with slightly rounded corners or an overall rounded style is generally best.

OBLONG

The oblong face is long but not square. It needs both width and angles. Choose slightly wide frames with rounded sides and straight bottoms to add shape. Choose largish glasses with heavier sides.

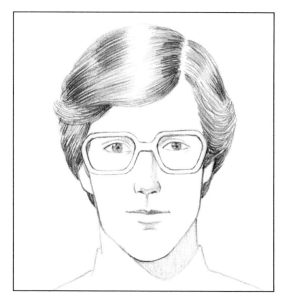

TRIANGLE

Since the triangular face has a broad forehead and narrow chin, you want glasses that create balance. The top piece of the frames should not be heavy, and the sides should not be wider than your temples. Consider glasses with a curved, dropped bottom piece, such as an aviator frame. Square shapes are out, as is a heavy bridge.

ACCENTUATE THE POSITIVE: Once you have determined the general frame shape that is best for you, you can refine it even further to accentuate your best features and disguise your flaws.

- *If you have a long nose,* choose glasses with a low bridge. A dark-colored bridge is even more shortening.
- *If you have a short nose,* a high, keyhole bridge in a light color lengthens the appearance of your nose.
- *If your eyes are small or too close together,* make them appear wider with a wide bridge. A clear bridge with colored end pieces makes the illusion even stronger.
- *If your nose is wide or your eyes are wide set,* choose a medium-weight dark-colored bridge.

GROOMING

Please don't forget the details that ensure your attractiveness as a total person. Good grooming is key to a successful image. Here's a grooming checklist:

1. Hair clean and neat.
2. Teeth brushed; good breath.
3. Deodorant—make sure it's still working.
4. Face shaved. (Watch for five o'clock shadow. Keep a razor at work.)
5. Fingernails clean and filed; cuticles trimmed. (It's easy to get a manicure each time you get a haircut.)
6. Clothes clean, neatly pressed. (Check for hanging threads, loose buttons, sagging lining, and split seams.)
7. Shirt cuffs and collars without frays.
8. Shoes polished, heels not worn.

Color for Men is a total concept.

You now have the tools to buy the best colors and clothing styles for you as well as a more organized approach to getting dressed.

Mix that with a great haircut, a neat and clean appearance, and you've got it all. Ready, set, go, put your best look forward!

THE TOTAL MAN

Throughout this book we have stressed the outer you—your appearance, your image, your looks. But the true results of applying your colors are inner. The harmony and self-confidence that come with being comfortable with your appearance make you feel good. And self-esteem is what life is all about, for your own special qualities are what really make you valuable in your business life and inspire affection in your personal life. Knowing that you look your best gives you the freedom and the confidence to continue to develop your full potential.

So here's to the Total Man! Enjoy your colors!

SHOPPING GUIDE FOR A WINTER MAN

Neutrals	Lights	Basic Colors	Brights/Accents	
Navy	Pure White	True Blue	Royal Blue	True Red
Black	Icy Gray	Pine Green	Hot Turquoise	Shocking Pink
Taupe (Gray-Beige)	Icy Blue	Bright Burgundy	Chinese Blue	Deep Hot Pink
Charcoal Gray	Icy Yellow	Blue-Red	Lemon Yellow	Magenta
Medium True Gray	Icy Pink		Light True Green	Fuchsia
Light True Gray	Icy Green		True Green	Royal Purple
	Icy Violet		Emerald Green	
	Icy Aqua			

Suits, Pants
Select suits and pants from your Neutral group. Neutrals form the foundation of your wardrobe because they go with everything.

Patterns: Winters are best in solids or pinstripes that offer sharp contrasts.

Business/Dress Shirts
Choose business and dress shirts from the Lights category. Wear them as solids or with stripes or checks from any of your color groups (example: White shirt with Bright Burgundy stripe). Shirt colors are important, since they are worn next to the face.

Casual Clothes
Casual clothes and sportswear may be worn in Brights/Accents as solids or in stripes or other prints, according to your personality. Here's your chance to add a new dimension to your casual wardrobe.

Sport Coats
Select sport coats from the Basic Color or Neutral groups. Basic Colors are the ones that are versatile, go with many of your other colors, and add interest to your wardrobe.

Ties
Ties can bring life to your overall appearance. Select colors from any group that relate to your shirt and coat—Neutrals or Basic Colors for a more conservative look. Winters are best in solids or contrasting stripes, but can also wear polka dots or foulards that contain some sharpness.

Shoes and Belts
Black, Navy, Cordovan, and Gray are the appropriate colors here. For warm weather, add Taupe or White.

Overcoat
Choose Black, Navy, Gray, or Taupe (Gray-Beige), whichever is your best.

SHOPPING GUIDE FOR A WINTER MAN

Name _____

Address _____

_____

SHOPPING REMINDER
(List Sizes)

Shirt: Neck _____ Sleeve _____

Sport shirt: S   M   L   XL

Suit/Jacket _____

Waist: _____

Pant length: _____

Sock: _____

Shoe: _____

Glove: _____

Overcoat: _____

Other: _____

Enjoy your colors!

SHOPPING GUIDE FOR A SUMMER MAN

Neutrals	Lights	Basic Colors	Brights/Accents	
Grayed Navy	Soft White	Cadet Blue	Light Lemon	Pastel Pink
Charcoal Blue-	Light Rose-Beige	Burgundy	Yellow	Rose-Pink
Gray	Powder Blue	Blue-Red	Sky Blue	Deep Rose
Light Blue-Gray	Light Periwinkle	Spruce Green	Medium Blue	Orchid
Grayed Blue	Blue		Periwinkle Blue	Mauve
Rose-Brown	Pale Lemon		Pastel Aqua	Raspberry
Cocoa	Yellow		Pastel Blue-Green	Soft Fuchsia
Rose-Beige	Powder Pink		Medium Blue-	Plum
	Light Mauve		Green	
	Lavender		Deep Blue-Green	
			Watermelon Red	

Suits, Pants
Select suits and pants from your Neutral group. Neutrals form the foundation of your wardrobe because they go with everything.

Patterns: Summers are best in solids or subtle patterns that offer minimal contrast.

Sport Coats
Select sport coats from the Basic Color or Neutral groups. Basic Colors are the ones that are versatile, go with many of your other colors, and add interest to your wardrobe.

Business/Dress Shirts
Choose business and dress shirts from the Lights category. Wear them as solids, or with stripes or checks from any of your color groups (example: Soft White shirt with Blue stripe). Shirt colors are important, since they are worn next to the face.

Ties
Ties can bring life to your overall appearance. Select colors from any group that relate to your shirt and coat—Neutrals or Basic Colors for a more conservative look. Summers are best in subtle patterns—foulards, small dots, blended stripes.

Shoes and Belts
Rose-Brown, Black, Navy, Cordovan, and Gray are the appropriate colors here. For warm weather, add Rose-Beige or Soft White.

Casual Clothes
Casual clothes and sportswear may be worn in Brights/Accents as solids or in stripes or other prints, according to your personality. Here's your chance to add a new dimension to your casual wardrobe.

Overcoat
Choose Navy, Grayed Blue, Rose-Brown, or Cocoa, whichever is your best.

SHOPPING GUIDE FOR A SUMMER MAN

Name _____

Address _____

_____

SHOPPING REMINDER
(List Sizes)

Shirt: Neck _____Sleeve _____

Sport shirt: S   M   L   XL

Suit/Jacket _____

Waist: _____

Pant length: _____

Sock: _____

Shoe: _____

Glove: _____

Overcoat: _____

Other: _____

Enjoy your colors!

SHOPPING GUIDE FOR AN AUTUMN MAN

Neutrals	Lights	Basic Colors		Brights/Accents	
Charcoal Brown	Oyster White	Forest Green	Yellow-Gold	Bittersweet Red	
Dark Chocolate	Warm Beige	Medium Warm	Mustard	Dark Tomato Red	
Brown	Buff (Light Gold)	Bronze	Pumpkin	Jade Green	
Coffee Brown	Light Peach/	Rust	Terra-Cotta	Lime Green	
Khaki/Tan	Apricot	Mahogany	Deep Peach/	Moss Green	
Camel	Light Periwinkle	Gold	Apricot	Bright Yellow-	
Marine Navy	Blue	Teal Blue	Salmon	Green	
Olive Green	Light Grayed		Orange	Turquoise	
Grayed Green	Green		Orange-Red	Deep Periwinkle	
				Blue	

Suits, Pants

Select suits and pants from your Neutral group. Neutrals form the foundation of your wardrobe because they go with everything.

Patterns: Autumns are often best in tweeds, plaids, and rich, nubby fabrics.

Business/Dress Shirts

Choose business and dress shirts from the Lights category. Wear them as solids or with stripes or checks from any of your color groups (example: Oyster White shirt with Rust stripe). Shirt colors are important, since they are worn next to the face.

Casual Clothes

Casual clothes and sportswear may be worn in Brights/Accents as solids or in stripes or other prints, according to your personality. Here's your chance to add a new dimension to your casual wardrobe.

Sport Coats

Select sport coats from the Basic Color or Neutral groups. Basic Colors are the ones that are versatile, go with many of your other colors, and add interest to your wardrobe.

Ties

Ties can bring life to your overall appearance. Select colors from any group that relate to your shirt and coat—Neutrals or Basic colors for a more conservative look. Autumns are best with rich colors worn in paisleys, plaids, irregular stripes, or foulards.

Shoes and Belts

Brown, Cordovan, Black (with navy), and Tan are the appropriate colors here. For warm weather, add Beige or Oyster.

Overcoat

Choose Charcoal Brown, Coffee, Khaki/Tan, Camel, or Marine Navy, whichever is your best

SHOPPING GUIDE FOR AN AUTUMN MAN

Name _____

Address _____

_____

SHOPPING REMINDER
(List Sizes)

Shirt: Neck _____Sleeve _____

Sport shirt: S   M   L   XL

Suit/Jacket _____

Waist: _____

Pant length: _____

Sock: _____

Shoe: _____

Glove: _____

Overcoat: _____

Other: _____

Enjoy your colors!

SHOPPING GUIDE FOR A SPRING MAN

Neutrals	Lights	Basic Colors	Brights/Accents	
Clear Bright Navy	Ivory	Light Clear Navy	Pastel Yellow-	Medium Violet
Medium Warm	Buff	Light Clear Gold	Green	Bright Golden
Gray	Light Peach/	Light Rust	Bright Yellow-	Yellow
Light Warm Gray	Apricot	Light Teal Blue	Green	Peach/Apricot
Chocolate Brown	Warm Pastel Pink		Light Warm Aqua	Clear Salmon
Medium Golden	Light Clear Blue		Clear Bright Aqua	Clear Bright Warm
Brown	Light Periwinkle		Emerald	Pink
Golden Tan	Blue		Turquoise	Coral Pink
Camel			Light True Blue	Bright Coral
Light Warm Beige			Periwinkle Blue	Light Orange
			Dark Periwinkle	Orange-Red
			Blue	Clear Bright Red

Suits, Pants

Select suits and pants from your Neutral group. Neutrals form the foundation of your wardrobe because they go with everything.

Patterns: Springs are often best in glen plaids or solids with a slight texture.

Sport Coats

Select sport coats from the Basic Color or Neutral groups. Basic Colors are the ones that are versatile, go with many of your other colors, and add interest to your wardrobe.

Business/Dress Shirts

Choose business and dress shirts from the Lights category. Wear them as solids or with stripes or checks from any of your color groups (example: Ivory shirt with Blue stripe). Shirt colors are important, since they are worn next to the face.

Ties

Ties can bring life to your overall appearance. Select colors from any group that relate to your shirt and coat—Neutrals or Basic Colors for a more conservative look. Springs are best in solids or subtle prints: plaids, stripes, foulards.

Shoes and Belts

Brown, Tan, Cordovan, and Black (with navy) are the appropriate colors here. For warm weather, add Beige and Ivory.

Casual Clothes

Casual clothes and sportswear may be worn in Brights/Accents as solids or in stripes or other prints, according to your personality. Here's your chance to add a new dimension to your casual wardrobe.

Overcoat

Choose Camel, Medium Warm Gray, Golden Tan, or Light Clear Navy, whichever is your best.

SHOPPING GUIDE FOR A SPRING MAN

Name _____

Address _____

_____

SHOPPING REMINDER
(List Sizes)

Shirt: Neck _____ Sleeve _____

Sport shirt: S   M   L   XL

Suit/Jacket _____

Waist: _____

Pant length: _____

Sock: _____

Shoe: _____

Glove: _____

Overcoat: _____

Other: _____

Enjoy your colors!

Fabric Glossary

Here are some examples of common menswear fabric patterns.

Tweed

Tic Weave

⅛″ Pinstripe

¼″ Pinstripe

Fabric Glossary

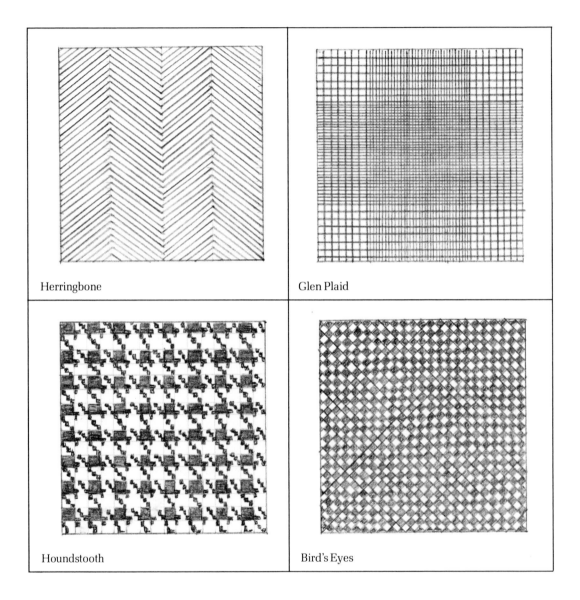

Herringbone

Glen Plaid

Houndstooth

Bird's Eyes

INDEX

CREDITS

Thanks to the following models for their participation: Terry Applebee (Panache) pp. 18, 19, 30; Joe Banks (Panache) p. 27; Steve Black, p. 30; Neil Bonin (Panache) p. 27; John Bracken (Zoli) p. 39; Arthur Brooks (Funny Face) pp. 19, 20, 35; William Fitzgerald, p. 31; Joe Flemming (Central Casting) p. 38; Jay Gould (Wilhelmina) p. 34; Addison Greene (Funny Face) p. 34; John Healy (Central Casting) p. 31; Tim Horan (International Legends) p. 38; Bob Jundelin (Funny Face) pp. 17, 20, 39; Mel Jurden (Funny Face) p. 31; Tim Kelley, p. 27; Calvin Kirby (Central Casting) p. 39; Lowell McGlothian (Ford Models) p. 38; J.R. Moyers, p. 35; Billy O'Briant (Panache) p. 31; Steve Puchaski (Wilhelmina) p. 30; Gordon Ramsey (Funny Face) p. 30; Stephen Reeder, p. 34; John Rusnak (Panache) p. 34; Dale Schusterman, p. 27; Ben Short (Funny Face) p. 26; Jacques Silberstein, pp. 17, 18; Dan S. Smith (Panache) p. 26; John Smith, p. 39; Richard Smith (Ford Models) p. 35; Toshio Soto (Funny Face) p. 26; Rick Spates (Funny Face) p. 38; Dale Stephenson (Panache) p. 35; Dean Vernon (Funny Face) p. 26

Photos by Jacques Silberstein (except J.R. Moyers, photo by David Neely). Grooming by Anne Schwab's Model Store (Washington, D.C.) and Bill Westmoreland (N.Y.C.).

Thanks to the following designers and stores for providing the clothing for the photographs in this book: Etienne Aigner; Bacarrat for Van Heusen Designer Group; Peter Barton's Closet; Geoffrey Beene; Britches of Georgetown; D. Cenci, New York; Country Britches; Cricketeer; Eagle Shirt Makers; Alan Flusser; Henry Grethel; Hathaway; Hennessy for Van Heusen Designer Group; Alexander Julian; Calvin Klein; Lacoste; Ted Lapidus; Ralph Lauren; Mano-A-Mano, New York; Saks Fifth Avenue, Chevy Chase; Van Heusen Designer Group

COLOR FOR MEN™

If you would like to purchase a set of fabric swatches in your season's colors with a checkbook-style carrying case, write or call for information:

Carole Jackson
P. O. Box 3241
Falls Church, VA 22043

In the United States (except Virginia): 800-533-5503
In Virginia: 800-572-2335
In Canada: 1-800-633-1010

If you would like the names of Color for Men consultants nearest you, or information on how to become a consultant, call or write to the address above.